THE FALSE EX

HOW TO E
(AND S

CW01621831

JOHN LAMERTON

COPYRIGHT

Title: The False EXIT: How To Exit Your Business (And Still Own It!)

First published in 2023

Address: Big Idea Books, PO Box 74, Plymouth, Devon, PL7 1ZN

The author specifically disclaims any liability, loss or risk which is incurred as a consequence, directly or indirectly, of the use and application of any contents of this work.

ISBN: 978-1-915222-01-5 (Paperback)
ISBN: 978-1-915222-02-2 (hardcover)

Book Interior and E-book Design by AmitDey | amitdey2528@gmail.com

This guide is not endorsed by or affiliated with any other website or organisation mentioned in this book in any way.

CONTENTS

INTRODUCTION

"Thinking to get at once all the gold the goose could give, he killed it and opened it, only to find nothing."

– Aesop's Fables,
The Goose that Laid the Golden Eggs

DO YOU OWN YOUR BUSINESS OR DOES YOUR BUSINESS OWN YOU?

If you're looking to cash in your golden goose and sail off into the sunset, this probably isn't the book for you.

You see, this isn't a book about selling your business. This is a book about *not* selling your business. It's about nurturing your golden goose, rather than killing it.

In fact, you'll learn how to turn your business into a factory that reliably produces golden eggs on a regular basis, but doesn't require you to work on the production line.

A False EXIT removes the business owner from the front line – no longer running the business, but instead owning and optimising it. Instead of being the boss, the gaffer, the MD, the CEO, the godlike genius through which everything runs (and without whom nothing runs!), you'll become the majority shareholder and chief architect of your business.

I'll level with you. I'm not actually very good at running businesses.

That may seem like a strange statement for someone who's been involved in more than 60 small businesses over the course of a couple of decades, and written several books for small business owners. But that's my point – I'm pretty damn good at being a small business *owner*, but I'm a terrible small business *runner*.

I'm an appalling leader. I avoid going into the office and only speak with my team once or twice a week. I detest giving speeches, leading meetings or all the other CEO-y stuff at which your business heroes excel. To make matters worse, I spend most of my time not working. I home-school my kids, look after my elderly parents, go to the gym, and enjoy long dog walks in nature.

After those things are taken care of – and only after – I allocate whatever time remains to work. I work to live, not live to work.

Go on, say it. I know you're thinking it and you're right. By conventional terms, I'm lazy. I won't deny it. I am lazy. I don't want to run businesses, I want to own businesses that run themselves. I became known as "the lazy entrepreneur" after the opening line of my first book *Big Ideas... for Small Businesses*, which read: "I hate being busy. I'm the laziest ambitious person I know."

I used to worry that my laziness was my Achilles heel. I'd see my entrepreneurial friends hustle their way to multi-million-pound exits or significant six-figure salaries and try to imitate them – without success. So, instead of pushing treacle uphill, working myself into the ground, I just hired people to do the stuff I hated and spent my time building automated systems to replace me – doing the work once, and reaping the rewards again and again.

It felt like cheating. I'd found a way to balance my ambition (owning more than 60 small businesses, earning very good money) with my laziness ("working" an average of 20 hours per week with ten weeks of holiday a year).

Many of my hustler friends now have millions of pounds in the bank. Nice, right? Well, unfortunately, a great deal of them also have failed marriages, significant health problems, and an unhealthy obsession with money. Could it be that my so-called laziness is actually a huge advantage?

False EXIT-style laziness doesn't mean you'll spend all day on the golf course or sip cocktails in Barbados as part of a four-hour work week. Instead, you'll take a step back from the day-to-day operations, becoming an observer of your business rather than its operator. You'll learn to let go of the reins and lean on your team.

Many small business owners (and I include myself in this generalisation) struggle to let go. You've created this little world in which everything works exactly the way you want. The minute you let go of the wheel, your business suddenly feels like an out of control car, destined to swerve into a ditch or a tree and burst into flames unless, at the very last minute, you grab the steering wheel again and take back full control.

As a result, this is where most small businesses remain. In 2021, there were an estimated 5.5million small businesses in the UK, and 4.2million of them (76%) had no employees at all. Perhaps you're one of those one-person bands. Maybe you tried hiring someone in the past, and when that person didn't behave exactly as you would, you snatched the steering wheel back. After this happened a few times, you said to yourself: "I'm the only one who can do this. I wish I could just clone myself!"

I've met many business owners like this. They've built up muscle memory over several years, convincing themselves that they are the only person capable of doing things properly, and that without their constant micro-management, their company will descend into chaos.

These types of people don't really own a business. Their business owns *them*.

What would happen to your business if you went on holiday for a month? If you think it would all fall apart, you've designed your business to rely on you, so it's back to the drawing board you go.

A False EXIT isn't about cloning you. It's about turning your business into a predictable machine, designed in your mould. Your team will never be you. They'll never think, behave or act exactly the way you do, because they're not you – there's only one you. Instead, it's about creating systems and processes that help your team to think and act like you. It's about coaching your team so they know why you think and act the way you do.

Once you've implemented what you'll learn in this book, you will own a business that doesn't rely on you, yet still benefits from your expertise and experience, your values and strategic input. You'll still own the golden goose – and it'll be a goose that won't keel over and die if you take a few weeks off.

PIPELINES, NOT BUCKETS

Once upon a time, there were two brothers, Barry and Paul. They were both dreamers, often talking late into the night about how, one day, they would become the richest men in town.

They were hard workers, always on the lookout for an opportunity. One day, the town mayor presented them with one. He said: "We're looking for two men to carry water from the river in the hills down to a cistern in the town square."

Paul immediately piped up: "Look no further, Mr Mayor. My brother Barry and I are just the men for the job!"

By sunrise the following morning, Barry and Paul were headed for the river, armed with a couple of buckets each. The brothers worked tirelessly throughout the day, lugging bucket after bucket of water down to the town centre, then turning around and trudging back up the steep hill to collect more.

At the end of the day, the mayor was ecstatic with the brothers' work and gave them a penny for each bucket of water they had successfully delivered. "Same again tomorrow morning, lads?" asked the mayor.

"You bet," smiled Barry. But Paul wasn't so sure. After a long day going up and down the hill ferrying heavy buckets, his back ached and his hands were blistered. The thought of getting up before dawn and doing the same thing day after day worried him greatly, and he went to bed that night dreaming of a better way to get the water from the river to the cistern.

"I've got a plan," Paul announced the next morning as the brothers grabbed their buckets and headed up towards the river. "Rather than spending all day breaking our backs lugging these buckets back and forth for a few pence, why don't we build a pipeline down from the river to the town centre?"

"Oh, I don't know about that," Barry replied. "We've got a great job here if we don't mess it up. I can carry more than 100 buckets a day. At a penny a bucket, I'm earning a pound a day here. I'm rich. This is the best gig in town. As long as we keep carrying buckets, we're set for life. Pah! You and your dreams. A pipeline, indeed."

But Paul wasn't to be discouraged. He agreed to help Barry carry buckets in the mornings, after which Paul would work on his pipeline in the afternoons and weekends. Now, Paul knew what he was getting into. He knew that carving out the route for his pipeline through the rocky soil would be back-breaking work. He also knew that, because he was paid by the bucket, his income would drop considerably and it may take a year or more before his pipeline was up and running. But Paul believed in his idea, and so set to work.

A few weeks later, Barry was spending his bucket-carrying money having lunch in a local pub when he spotted Paul hard at work digging trenches in the midday sun. "Oh look," one of the locals called out. "It's Pipeline Paul!" The whole bar collapsed in fits of laughter. Barry felt bad for Paul. He was earning twice as much money as his brother, who seemed to be working twice as hard. Try as he might, though, Barry couldn't dissuade Paul from building his pipeline.

While Barry rested his weary body each evening, and every weekend, Paul kept digging his pipeline. For months, Paul saw little progress. He inched forward, making tiny incremental gains. Day after day, he dug and dug and then dug some more. Eventually, inches turned into feet. Feet became yards, and, after several months of gruelling spadework, Paul's pipeline – which began high in the hills – reached halfway to the town centre.

Paul now only had to carry his buckets half as far as Barry, enabling him to earn the same money as his brother in half the time – time he put to good use, accelerating his pipeline project, further compounding his gains. Paul was now able to take regular breaks, during which he would cast pitiful looks at his brother Barry, who continued to lug buckets all the way from the river to the cistern, one at a time, before pausing, pain etched on his face, as he stooped to lift yet another bucket to earn one more penny.

Many times, Paul offered Barry the chance to join his pipeline project, but each time, his brother refused. "I can't afford to do that," he complained. "If I don't carry buckets, I don't get paid."

Eventually, the big day arrived and Paul's pipeline was finally complete. The community crowded around as water flowed naturally all the way from the river to the cistern without a single bucket needed. With a constant, reliable source of fresh water on demand, people from all over the countryside moved into the town, creating evermore demand for fresh water – leading to Paul earning not just from the 100 buckets of water he could physically carry each day, but the thousands his pipeline could deliver.

Paul's dreams didn't stop there. He had a vision of building pipelines into towns and villages all over the country. Even Barry's bucket-carrying days were now behind him. Instead, the two brothers worked on building pipelines together – one digging while the other followed behind laying the pipework.

Laying the foundations for your own False EXIT is going to be hard work. It will take a long time. And you'll have to make some sacrifices in the short term. But, just like Pipeline Paul, you'll reap the rewards in the long term by building pipelines rather than carrying buckets.

1. HOW WILL *YOU* GET OUT?

"In this world nothing can be said to be certain, except death and taxes,"

– Benjamin Franklin

How will you exit your business? I mean, you will have to leave it one day and if you haven't got an exit plan then it'll likely happen in one of two ways – you will die or your business will die.

Sorry to be so morbid, but those are the facts. If their business doesn't croak it first, most business owners exit feet first in a box. They keep running the business until the day they die and often the business dies with them. Researchers found, on average, the death of a founder wipes out 60% of a firm's sales and cuts jobs by around 17%. The disparity between those two figures tells its own story about how much those firms relied on their owner.

Two years after the founder's death, these companies have a 20% lower survival rate, and even four years after the business owner has shuffled off this mortal coil, most firms show no sign of ever recovering. So much for "leaving it to the kids".

Let's assume that you don't die (yet!) and your business doesn't either. If there's no pre-existing exit plan, what's going to be the trigger that would cause you to suddenly want to exit?

Well, if you're like most owners, you'll keep running the business until you burn out, have an "I can't do this anymore" moment, and then throw your toys out of the pram. Then you'll scramble around, desperately hunting for someone to relieve you of the burden that your business has become – ultimately selling it on the cheap or foisting it onto a family member. Anything to avoid Frankenstein's Monster.

"But, John, I never want to exit my business. I love what I do, and do what I love!" That's great, but you're still going to exit one day (unless you've discovered the secret to immortality), and while you may well love what you do right now, very few things stay the same forever and there's no guarantee you're still going to love it in a few years.

STOP CRYING YOUR HEART OUT

Paul McGuigan grew up in Manchester in the 1980s. Inspired by the Madchester scene, which saw bands such as the Stone Roses and Happy Mondays rise to fame, Paul started a band, The Rain, with his mates Paul Arthurs, Chris Hutton and Tony McCarroll.

After lead singer Hutton was sacked from the band, Paul invited one of his old school pals to replace him. That schoolmate was Liam Gallagher. Liam brought along his brother Noel, changed the band's name to Oasis, and the rest, some might say, is history.

Suddenly, Paul (or Guigsy as he became better known) was transported from jamming with his mates and playing to a handful of people in tiny pubs to being part of the biggest band in the world. They were now travelling the globe, selling millions of albums, having their faces plastered all over every newspaper and playing gigs to 125,000 people a night at Knebworth.

What kid just starting out in a band doesn't want this?

Paul McGuigan, that's who. Guigsy never wanted to be famous. He just liked playing bass guitar. After a few years of "hiding in the back" of Oasis, he had earned more money than he would ever know what to do with. The thought of spending months away from home touring, and dealing with Liam and Noel's evermore-public fallouts, was becoming less and less appealing.

Actor Bill Murray once said: "I always want to say to people who want to be rich and famous: Try being rich first. See if that doesn't cover most of it. There's not much downside to being rich, other than paying taxes and having your relatives ask you for money. But when you become famous, you end up with a 24-hour job."

As a kid, Paul signed up for fame and fortune. By the time he was 28, he had all the fortune he would ever need and far more fame than he ever wanted. So, in 1999, at the peak of their success, Guigsy quietly faxed his resignation to the band and proceeded to slide away into obscurity – his dream lifestyle:

> *"Whilst I was in Oasis, I was very fortunate to have had a low profile and I always tried to hide away during videos, photoshoots, etc. Since leaving the band, I've been lucky enough to have faded back into anonymity."*

Noel Gallagher once joked that being in Oasis was a "lowly fifth" on Guigsy's list of favourite things after "cricket, Doctor Who, weed, and Manchester City".

Paul didn't want to be in the world's biggest band, so he orchestrated his own False EXIT – no longer carrying buckets day-to-day by recording in the studio or spending months touring the world, but still enjoying his pipeline share of the royalties from the band's first four albums.

All the upsides of fortune, with none of the demands of fame. Noel and Liam can't pop to the corner shop without being mobbed by fans wanting autographs and selfies, while most of us would walk past Guigsy in the street, oblivious that he was once part of a band described (by Noel) as "bigger than The Beatles".

Even if you believe you'll never want to exit your business, remember one thing: businesses change. They evolve. They grow (and shrink). The business you love right now may well turn into a business you hate in the future. When Paul asked his mate Liam to join The Rain, he couldn't in his wildest dreams have imagined what would happen to the band just a few short years later.

DO YOU WANT $273BILLION WITH THAT?

Have a guess who said this:

> *"See that big white house with a wide front porch? That's our home and we love it.*
>
> *We sit out on the porch in the evenings and watch the sunset and look down on our place here. It's peaceful.*
>
> *We don't need any more problems. We are in a position to enjoy life now. And that's just what we intend to do."*

They are the words of Mac McDonald, co-founder of McDonald's, when he first met milkshake mixer salesman Ray Kroc. Mac and his brother Dick had established a base of six restaurants across California, and Kroc wanted to convince the McDonald brothers to scale up to 1,000 restaurants throughout the United States.

Mac and Dick loved their little business. They didn't want to exit. They "didn't need any more problems", and intended to just "enjoy life now". But, like Liam and Noel joining The Rain, once Ray Kroc was involved with McDonald's, the brothers' business would never be the same again.

Kroc joined McDonald's as their franchise agent in 1954. Four years later, McDonald's opened its 100th restaurant, and sold its 100millionth hamburger. From six restaurants to 100 in just four years. So much for enjoying life on the porch, watching the sunset.

In 1961, Mac and Dick sold the rights to the McDonald's name for $2.7million, leaving each brother with $1million after tax (that's worth about $10million in today's money). Not bad for a little six-restaurant operation, right?

However, at the time of writing, all-time sales for McDonald's stands at a colossal $273*billion*. Had Mac and Dick opted for a False EXIT – leaving the day-to-day, bucket-carrying operations to Kroc and simply retained their pipeline 0.5% franchise fee on food sales – they (or their families) would have netted $1.365billion to date, with the figure rising considerably each day.

That's significantly more than the sum they received from their "traditional" exit in 1961. A couple of million dollars instead of £1.365billion – now that's leaving money on the table.

You will exit your business at some point, whether that be through death, business failure, burnout, black swans, boredom, or simply not enjoying it any more. Doesn't it make sense to at least consider how you want it to happen?

CAN YOU GET OUT?

Each year, I give away a 4ft high inflatable pink flamingo to a member of the One Percent Club, my group coaching platform for small business owners. The Pink Flamingo Award goes to the One Percenter who has spent the most complete days *not* running their business.

One recipient was Michele Marsland, an accountant who spent most of January (self-assessment season) sunning herself in Tenerife, and only worked a few hours a week the rest of the year.

Why an inflatable flamingo?

It all started after a One Percent Club coaching call with guest Gerald Ratner. He was there to tell us how he'd built Britain's largest high-street jewellers, Ratners, with annual sales in excess of £1billion – before losing it all after telling this joke in a speech at the Royal Albert Hall in 1991:

> *"We do cut-glass sherry decanters with six glasses on a silver-plated tray that your butler can serve you drinks on for £4.95. People say, 'How can you sell this for such a low price?'. I say, 'Because it's total crap'."*

Overnight, the Press turned on Gerald with headlines such as: "JEWELLERY CEO CALLS OWN PRODUCTS 'CRAP'", "CRAPNERS", and "YOU 22-CARAT MUGS".

Within a few days, £500million had been wiped off the market value of Ratners and Gerald was eventually forced out of the company that his father had started in 1949.

In our coaching call, Gerald told us how he rebuilt his self-esteem and his empire – becoming a multi-millionaire again – enjoying newfound success as a public speaker, and also discovering a renewed sense of fulfilment and happiness in his personal life.

While all this was happening, however, my eye was drawn to the Zoom window next to Gerald, where One Percenter Ian Bluck had dialled into the call while on holiday with his family in Lanzarote. Had Ian found a quiet bar to connect to the call or a spot in reception? Was there a business centre at his hotel or had he simply dialled in from his room?

Nope. Ian was coming to us live from the poolside. There were kids splashing and jumping in the water. Ian himself was shirtless, sitting under a parasol next to a giant inflatable pink flamingo.

In that moment, it became the official symbol of the One Percent Club, and the idea for the Pink Flamingo Award was born. There aren't many places you'll find someone who built a billion-pound business, has had lunch with the Prime Minister, and can tell you what it feels like to earn £800,000 a year (in the 1980s), sitting next to a bloke in swim shorts with a 4ft inflatable flamingo.

But egos get left at the door on these coaching calls. Everyone taking part is serious about building their own ambitious, lifestyle business – whatever that means to them.

For some, it's family holidays (complete with inflatables). For others, it's early retirement, playing golf when it's sunny, or simply going for a meal with loved ones. When we asked Gerald Ratner what makes him happy nowadays, he didn't mention his car, house, stock portfolio or latest holiday destination.

No, he spoke instead of a love of great coffee, listening to his favourite music, and having the freedom to spend the day riding his bike in the countryside. The mic drop for me, though, was a casual aside at the end of the call. Gerald said his son was in town and they were heading out for a curry together, simply adding: "I wouldn't have been able to do that if I was still running Ratners."

Gerald Ratner didn't choose to exit Ratners. That choice was made for him. If you're the majority shareholder in your own small business, then deciding whether to exit should be under your control (barring health or business failures). But there's still one question you need to ask yourself: Can you exit your business?

If you're anything like me, you've probably spent a significant amount of time building your business. In some way, you've had a hand in all the processes, each piece of marketing, and absolutely everything your business touches. Your DNA runs through the company. It's *your* company, just the way you like it.

This can be a blessing as well as a curse because while you've built your business in your own likeness, you've also created a monster – one which relies entirely on you. Without you, nothing happens. Nothing works. Everything falls apart.

> *"I just wish I could clone myself."*
>
> *"No one can do it as well as me."*
>
> *"Every time I take a day off, I have to spend two more days putting out fires!"*

Have you ever uttered any of these sentences or something similar? Of course you have, you're a small business owner. Those are practically our catchphrases.

They're also a clear indication of one undeniable, uncomfortable truth: your business – as it stands – relies on *you*. It cannot and will not function without you. Take a day off and you'll have fires to put out when you return. Take a year off and you won't have a business to return to.

Consider for a moment whether you own a business or have a self-employed job.

You work for yourself. You call the shots. No one tells you what to do or how to do it. Great news – you're the boss.

But what happens when you stop working for a couple of days, a few weeks, or – Heaven forbid! – a few months? What happens to your business then? Do the sales dry up because nobody else likes making sales calls? Do you slowly bleed towards bankruptcy because you're the only person who understands the numbers? Do customers ring your mobile phone, write to your email address, and refuse to buy unless they've spoken to you?

It's simple: if you don't earn when you don't work, you don't own a business – you have a self-employed job where you've made yourself an irreplaceable bottleneck. If we're going to get you out of the business, we need to change that. The only way I know to exit a self-employed job is to close the door behind you, walk away with nothing, or find someone who will buy your self-employed job. And believe me, self-employed jobs where you have to carry your own buckets don't sell for anywhere near as much money as established pipeline businesses.

I used to be an angel investor in small businesses (I'm not anymore as it's far too much hard work for my ideal lifestyle). One day, a restaurant came onto my radar. I visited a few times and met with the owner, who on the face of it was living a great lifestyle. He drove a brand new Mercedes and had a villa in Greece, all paid for by the profits from the restaurant.

However, because he'd optimised the business around the lifestyle he wanted, his business was unsellable. His accounts showed a profit of just £26,500 a year. Of course, he assured me it was a lot more than that, with plenty of "cash deals" (also known as tax evasion and quite illegal). The owner took a small tax-efficient salary of £12,000 per year.

The restaurateur wanted £180,000 for his business – nearly seven times his declared annual profit. His asking price was based on the cash deals and, crucially, also valued his time (80 hours a week managing the entire restaurant and bar) at zero.

I explained I was only able to offer around £75,000 – roughly three times the profits actually declared to HMRC – and only if he could tell me where I could find a food and beverage manager with decades of experience willing to work for £2.88 an hour.

"I don't understand," he protested. "Why £2.88 an hour?"

"Well," I explained. "You're currently managing everything here, right? Front of house? The bar upstairs? The kitchen?"

"Yeah, that's right."

"And you're here from 2pm until midnight, Sunday to Thursday, and 5am on Friday and Saturday nights?"

"Most weeks, yes."

"And looking at the accounts here, I see you're paid a salary of £12,000."

"Ah yes, but you see the cash…"

I interrupted and told him that if I was to invest in the restaurant as a business – rather than become a self-employed barman, chef, waiter and pot washer myself – then I would need to employ a manager to do what he was currently doing. Furthermore, to ensure the business remains profitable, I could pay that person no more than £12,000 a year.

I told him: "For what you're working, that's £2.88 per hour. Do you know any highly experienced food and beverage managers willing to work for significantly less than minimum wage?"

Needless to say, I didn't buy his business and nor did anyone else. Four years later, it's still up for sale. As the company's sole shareholder, this restaurant owner had created a fantastic self-employed lifestyle for himself. But as a saleable asset and exit-able business? I'm sorry, but he wasn't selling a pipeline business, he was selling a bucket-carrying job.

A False EXIT is about freedom. The freedom to ride your bike, listening to your favourite bands, full of really good coffee. The freedom to pop out for a curry with your son "just because".

The freedom to stop working weekends and no longer check emails after 6pm.

The freedom to take an actual holiday (without the laptop, having diverted your work phone elsewhere).

The freedom that will give you a better lifestyle, a better business and maybe – just maybe – a 4ft inflatable pink flamingo too.

2. WHAT'S YOUR EXIT?

"In all things – except love – start with the exit strategy. Prepare for the ending. Almost anything is easier to get into than out of."

– Kevin Kelly

Assuming you've got both a desire to exit and a business you could exit, what sort of exit is right for you?

In this detailed chapter, we'll consider four of the main options – full sale, partial sale, management buyout, and doing nothing – each with real-life examples, before we then move on to a fifth option, the False EXIT, in the next section.

So, without further ado…

OPTION 1: FULL SALE

You could take the traditional, well-worn path, and simply sell your business lock, stock and barrel. There are many advantages to this option:

- You'd get to sail off into the sunset (usually) with a nice big payday.
- You could benefit from Business Asset Disposal Relief, paying as little as 10% capital gains tax (at the time of writing) on the sale.
- Once you sign on the dotted line, you could be free of all responsibilities, and need never worry about the business ever again.

Sounds good, doesn't it?

Of course, if it were that easy, everyone would be doing it. There's a lot of work to be done. First, you have to prepare your business for sale. It has to be *sellable*. Then, you have to find a buyer – someone with pockets deep enough to pay the price tag.

My friend Adam has made these first few steps – creating a sellable business and marketing it to the right buyers – his entire business model. He once told me: "My business only has one customer – the person who's going to buy my business." For the rest of us, learning how to market a business to those who might buy it is something we'll either need to learn or outsource, usually to a business broker, who, of course, will want a slice of your pie.

Next, you will need to negotiate with the buyer because they won't want to buy a lemon, and you don't want to sell your baby for less than it's worth. By the way, most owners overvalue their business thanks to this "but it's my baby" mindset. Again, business brokers can negotiate for you but, just like an estate agent, their incentive isn't necessarily to maximise the sale price. It's simply to ensure a deal gets done, so they can earn their commission.

Next are two words that still strike fear into my heart 15 years after I sold my tiny "freebies" website to a publicly listed company – due diligence.

Due diligence is really just a checklist to ensure that both parties are clear as to what's included in the sale and what's not, as well as finding any skeletons that could be hiding in the closet.

However, my experience of due diligence involved two weeks working full time to assure our potential purchaser (or, more accurately, our purchaser's solicitor) that the sky wasn't falling, we didn't have Shergar and Lord Lucan tucked away somewhere, and the website wasn't a front for a Colombian drug lord. I'm joking – mostly.

What started as an exercise in crossing t's and dotting i's soon descended into Doomsday prepping, until eventually the buyer's CEO called me: "Can we stop the due diligence, John? You're a good guy, I'm a good guy. We've known each other for years. We both want to do this deal. We've done enough research to know what we're buying. Let's both tell our solicitors to back off and get the deal done."

So that's exactly what we did and exactly what happened. There were no skeletons in the closet and the buyers got what they were expecting. The only people that were unhappy were both of our lawyers, who missed a chance to extract more money out of the deal for themselves by writing snooty letters to each other.

Finally, once you've prepared your business for sale, marketed the business, found a buyer, negotiated terms, completed due diligence, and paid the solicitors, brokers, and taxman their slice of the pie, *then* you can pour yourself a pina colada and head to the golf course to spend (what's left of) your cheque.

Unless, of course, your buyer has insisted on an earn-out. In which case, you might be required to turn up for work again on Monday morning – indeed every morning – for the next few years, before getting your hands on the money. This greatly reduces the risk for the buyer, who is not required to hand over the bulk of the acquisition cost until:

1. The company has earned enough money to pay for its own acquisition.
2. Any risk that the company is a lemon is assumed by the seller (that's you, by the way).

To someone who has run their own business for years, the idea of finishing your career off by going back to being an employee can be hugely unappealing. The late Tony Hsieh, famous for selling online shoe retailer Zappos.com to Amazon for more than a billion dollars, cut his teeth on a slightly smaller deal. A decade earlier, he sold online advertising business LinkExchange to Microsoft for $265million. Hsieh personally received $40million upfront, with a further earn-out payment of $8million to be received once Tony had stayed with the business for 12 months.

However, Tony walked away from that $8million payday. In his autobiography *Delivering Happiness*, Hsieh wrote: "I wasn't going to sit around letting my life and the world pass me by. People thought I was crazy for giving up all that money. And, yes, making that decision was scary, but in a good way."

Even when you finally have (what's left of) the proceeds from selling your baby, what's next? Are you going to sit around letting your life and the world pass you by? What reason will you have for getting out of bed in the morning? Are you going to spend the rest of your life on the golf course? Or are you going to get right back out there and start your next company? Because there'll be no turning back once you've killed the golden goose.

WHO WANTS TO BE A MILLIONAIRE? MY FAILED FULL SALE EXIT...

"I think we can get you two million pounds."

Jason and I had driven to meet with a company that specialised in business exits. We weren't actively looking to sell our sports betting firm, but kept hearing "gurus" talking about the importance of an exit strategy, so we went out of polite curiosity.

Yet on the way back home, Jason and I mentally divided up our £2million, and planned to live out the rest of our lives on the golf course. We had no reason to sell the business on the drive up in the morning but by the evening, we had two million of them!

We instructed the brokers to proceed with marketing the business for sale and got to work deciding what our next cars would be and where we would moor our yachts.

However, the bubble burst within a week when I received a literal Dear John letter from the brokers:

> *"Dear John,*
>
> *It was a great pleasure meeting you and Jason last week and to hear more about your history in business and motives for exploring a potential sale.*
>
> *After every such meeting, we review each opportunity on its own merits, but in particular, we need to ensure that we can be confident of success before we can take you on as a client. In this instance, I'm afraid the consensus is that we do not possess the relevant experience in your market to be sure of finding a buyer.*
>
> *May I take the opportunity to wish you both every success in the future."*

With that, £2million we never had vanished. Like Chris Tarrant on Who Wants to Be a Millionaire, they'd waved a life-changing cheque at us, then snatched it back, saying: "But we don't want to give you that!" It's a good job we didn't order the yachts.

With the potential sale falling through before it even got started, we chose not to pursue a sale ourselves, because identifying and courting buyers, creating and delivering deal presentations, negotiations, and those two scary words – due diligence – would, once again, all be down to me.

Oh, the irony. In order to exit a business so it doesn't rely on me, the exit process relies entirely on me and I didn't have a clue what I was doing, so I left it well alone.

OPTION 2: PARTIAL SALE

Could you enjoy the best of both worlds? Sell part of your golden goose, enjoying a lump sum payday plus a share of all future profits? We've already seen how the McDonald brothers could have earned a load more cash by considering such an offer.

Felix Dennis – founder of Dennis Publishing, creator of titles such as Men's Fitness, MoneyWeek, and Viz, and with an estimated net worth at the time of his death of around £300million – has very clear views on diluting your shareholding:

> *"Never, never, never hand over a single share of anything you've created or acquired, if you can help it. Nothing. Not one share, to no one, no matter what the reason, unless you genuinely have to."*

I think it's pretty clear where Felix Dennis stood on partial ownership. And I have to say, I agree with him for the most part. Very rarely do I see small business owners sell a slice of their business and not regret it. They think they're bringing someone in to spread the load, to share the trials and tribulations, and cash in a little of their hard-earned equity at the same time.

Instead, like Ray Kroc versus the McDonald brothers, they end up with a partner who wants to take the business in a different direction. Suddenly, they find they're no longer in control of their baby and their success (and future income) is dictated by someone else. For "my way or the highway" control freak entrepreneurs like me, this can be devastating.

It's often just as bad for the new shareholder who's just bought in. They believe they're buying a slice of an established, successful business, one that they can add value and take to the next level, only to find that the incumbent owners are clinging onto their vision and strategy for the company, rebuffing all suggestions for anything different, proclaiming: "That won't work. We've always done it this way!"

A partial sale *can* work, but it's rare. I can count on one hand the number of successful partial sales I've seen over the last two decades.

"Are you under any stress at all?" – My failed partial exit...

The rise of my internet marketing business in the early 2000s was meteoric. In my first nine months, I earned £13.51. Nine months later, I was able to quit my day job and within the next year was earning six figures and on course for seven.

I thought I had the Midas touch. I was clearly a genius at this business malarkey and, as such, plotted my trajectory towards becoming a millionaire. That would happen within 12 months, I thought, and I'd have £10million in the bank a few years after. By the end of the decade, I'd have £100million. Easy.

Spoiler alert: that's not quite what happened.

Instead, I became stupendously overconfident. I went from me working alone in my spare bedroom to hiring a team of 15 working across two offices, all personally guaranteed by me. And because I was going to be a millionaire soon, I also bought my dream house and a new car.

And then, predictably, it began to fall apart. I stupidly thought that just increasing the size of the operation would increase the profits by the same amount. Wrong! Instead of making tens of thousands of pounds in profit every month, I was losing tens of thousands.

If I'd realised my mistake at the time and simply scaled the business back a little, I would have been fine. But I was a business genius, remember, and I thought I could find a way through. However, my only tactic was to work harder, so 100-hour weeks became standard. I'd go to bed at around 3am still trying to think of ways to save the business and, after a few hours of fitful sleep, I'd be back at it again, fuelled by coffee and microwave pizzas.

Nothing worked and soon I had to weigh up paying either the VAT bill or payroll that month because I couldn't afford to do both. All this took its toll on my health and I ended up in hospital under investigation for an unexplained rash all over my body.

"Are you under any stress at all?" the doctor asked. I laughed, and spent the next ten minutes having a free therapy session from a dermatologist. She diagnosed my rash as stress-related, the result of extremely high levels of cortisol in my body, suggesting that I was on the verge of a nervous breakdown. She advised me to take some time off work and to "stop worrying".

That was easier said than done, but she was right. I couldn't carry on as I had. So I took drastic action. I met with my management team and explained I would be leaving the company in six months and that I'd like them to run things for me in my absence.

In return, I would sign over 49% of the company to them free of charge. Yep, I was so desperate to escape the monster I'd created that I was willing to give away 49% of a company that, just a few years earlier, I'd have valued at several million pounds.

I announced my "retirement" to the industry press. I was 27 years old. People thought I'd truly made it –to retire at such a young age, I must have made millions, sold the golden goose and planned on living the high life.

Nope. The truth was I was running away from my business because I couldn't hack it any more. I'd fallen out of love with it.

You'll be pleased to know that the rash disappeared within a few weeks of my "retirement". I also began to sleep at night and was feeling human again. However, retirement only lasted a year as the business finally ran out of money and I had to either return or risk losing everything.

On my first day back, I had to make half the team redundant. To this day, that remains the single hardest thing I have had to do and, as a result, I avoided hiring again for years. But even that wasn't enough. I had to shut down projects we'd invested huge sums into, close both offices and make other cutbacks. People may have thought I was cold-hearted, but it was my name on the guarantees and me who would lose it all if the company failed.

My first failed attempt to exit left me with a clear lesson learned: abdication doesn't work.

OPTION 3: MANAGEMENT BUY OUT

Do you know who would be the perfect buyers for your business? A consortium of people who already know it inside out, would know from day one exactly how to run things and who could really hit the ground running.

Yes, I'm talking about your current team, either via a Management Buy Out or a sale to an employee-owned trust. There are plenty of advantages to this option – it's tax efficient for you as the seller, due diligence should be a formality and there's very little risk on either side because the team knows what they're buying and you know who you're selling to.

You don't need to spend any time or effort marketing the business to potential buyers and can often maximise your desired valuation, as your team will relish the continuity of secure jobs, the prospect of a share in the profits and the power of a real say in how the business is run.

Guy Singh-Watson, owner of Riverford Organic Farms (who we'll meet in detail later), considered his options for 12 years before settling on employee ownership.

He was determined not to let the business get into the hands of external shareholders and with none of his four children interested in following in his farming footsteps, employee ownership was the most attractive option. In 2018, Guy sold 74% of Riverford to an employee-owned trust to protect his business's values and ensure its independence – believing it to have benefits for both the staff and the business, including greater productivity, higher morale, and less debt.

He was right because in 2023 – while I was busy writing this book – he sold his remaining shares to the employee-owned trust. Guy said: "I do so happily, with no regrets, and in full confidence that collectively, co-owners, customers, and suppliers will make more of Riverford than my waning energy could."

But this path is not without its pitfalls. First and foremost, there's a huge difference between being an employee and being a business owner. Not everyone wants to own the business – many people value being able to clock off at 5pm each evening and leave work at work until the next day. They don't want the added weight of being responsible for other people's livelihoods, the company's success depending on their decisions or dealing with all the red tape. They just want to turn up, do their job and go home.

Making them shareholders in the business isn't going to make them think or act like business owners overnight. And if everyone becomes a shareholder, then suddenly, everyone wants a say in everything the company does. Before you know it, all decisions are made by committee rather than a meritocracy:

> *"I think we should change our Buy Now buttons to red."*
>
> *"But I prefer blue!"*

"Let's compromise on green."

"Green always reminds me of my nan's avocado bathroom. How about beige?"

(Meanwhile, the new website still doesn't get launched...)

Assuming your employees do fancy themselves as business owners, you then have to consider whether they can actually afford to buy the business. Your team is unlikely to have large piles of money lying around waiting for an acquisition opportunity to present itself. Collectively, they may be able to borrow against the company's assets to fund a purchase or you could even agree to fund the purchase yourself with the business effectively lending your team the money to buy the business, with repayments coming out of future profits.

A word of warning if you do go down this route: you're effectively becoming a money lender and putting up your golden goose, your baby, as collateral and then walking away, trusting others to keep the ship on course. If they happen to mess things up, they've put very little skin in the game, while you've risked everything.

A Mediocre MD – My failed Management Buy Out exit

Not long after that £2million cheque I mentioned earlier vanished into thin air, I heard some guru on a podcast proclaim that selling your business was for fools and it would be far better to instead employ a "mediocre MD" (his words) to run things for you.

By his reckoning, this would enable you to still own the golden goose, but let someone else worry about harvesting the eggs on a daily basis. Even if your mediocre managing director is only 80% as good as you, you'd still be better off thanks to the tax efficiency and predictability of future revenue.

At least that's the theory. Here's what happened in (my) reality.

Jason and I decided to use a head-hunting agency to find our new MD, asking for local candidates to make it easier to have regular face-to-face meetings with them. Our mistake was already made.

Instead of hunting for the right person for our company, what the head-hunter was actually doing was finding companies to foist his unemployed mates upon. As a result, the candidate list was poor.

We met with one, Diane, who had excelled in sales, led a small team and said she was familiar with direct response marketing, the key element of the business. She came across as likeable and knowledgeable on each of the three times we interviewed her. Our only concern was that she'd never run an entire company before, but – as the only real candidate – we gave her the job.

She would bring new ideas and inspiration to the business, dedicating herself full time rather than my part-time leadership. At worst, she would be a "mediocre MD", slightly less effective than me, but with an additional salary to cover.

For the first few months, it appeared that things were going great. "Everyone's really happy," Diane told us during our monthly board meetings. "The team is really loving all the changes and they're doing great work." Each month, Jason and I would run through the KPIs, give feedback on areas of concern, set and agree targets, and then leave her to it.

A month later, we'd reconvene only to learn that the KPIs were heading in the wrong direction, our areas of concern had been ignored, and our targets replaced with excuses. We were assured time and time again, however, that everyone was "really happy".

Everyone except me and Jason, of course. We weren't happy, as profits plunged more than 75% over the course of that first year.

And things came to a head when Jason and I started talking to a few of our team members privately.

Rob, our head of marketing, informed us that "Diane doesn't really like direct response marketing". It turns out, she had stopped them sending out anything with a deadline or a call to action, as well as any follow-up emails.

Everything that drove our sales had been ditched and she had got our head of marketing working on customer service instead.

Of course the KPIs looked terrible and targets weren't met, we'd employed someone who didn't like direct response marketing to run a direct response marketing company. Ultimately, Rob quit and we nearly lost another key member of staff, Lee, due to Diane's micro-managing. He'd been forced to do things her way, even if it took him away from vital metrics and KPIs.

I say we "almost" lost Lee because we took another course of action instead. We let Diane go immediately. Our "Mediocre MD" had turned out to be an abysmal one – and that was *our* fault. We took shortcuts in the recruitment process and hired someone likeable without checking references and just left her to it.

Once again, it was more abdication than delegation. We didn't even notice she'd banned direct response marketing (in a direct response marketing business!) for nearly a year.

As I returned from my latest failed escape attempt, I begrudgingly accepted that I would "never" be able to exit the business, that it will always rely on me. Every time I leave, it fails. Every time I return, it thrives. As Michael Corleone says in The Godfather Part III: "Just when I thought I was out, they pull me back in!"

OPTION 4: DO NOTHING

This is the path most small business owners take. However, there are only four ways to exit your business by doing nothing:

1. You'll exit your business feet-first, in a box. You'll just keep running it until you drop dead.
2. You'll close the doors and retire. You'll treat your business like a job, reach a certain age (or level of health) and walk away, closing the doors on your way out, receiving £0 capital value for your shareholding.
3. Your business will fail, and eject you. More than 300,000 businesses fail in the UK each year. If yours is one of them, you will be ejected, rather than exited, and you may still be liable for some of the company's debts.
4. You'll get a fairy tale ending. Out of the blue, someone will magically wave a large cheque at you. The only place this happens on a regular basis is in Hollywood movies.

Toys well and truly thrown out the pram – My failed Do Nothing exit:

"I'm sorry, I can't do this anymore!"

I stormed out of the meeting, leaving Jason open-mouthed and visibly shocked by my outburst. My wife Sarah, who is also our company secretary, was horrified too (and later asked whether she should document my tantrum in the minutes of the meeting).

It's fair to say that my eruption was out of character, out of the blue and out of order. But it had been building.

On that day, Jason and I had embarked on a spirited debate about the best course of action for one of our information marketing business's services. Jason thought we should do A, I thought B. He disagreed with me, and I with him. We went round in circles for ten minutes until – BAM! – my toys were thrown out the pram.

That was the trigger, but the seeds were sown a year before during our debacle with the mediocre MD.

While she was busy destroying our business, I was busy trying to salvage something from a number of bad investments – including a buy-to-let property that turned out to be "uninhabitable" and a "high net worth" scheme that ended up with me speaking to the Serious Fraud Office in a bid to find the particular puff of smoke that our cash had disappeared into.

I was also occupied by winding up some of the many businesses we'd launched that never achieved lasting success – the telesales company, the garden supplies subscription service and the funeral guide website.

Then we sacked our mediocre MD, which meant a return to the day-to-day operations on the info marketing business.

But that's not all. Having just finished writing my second book, *Routine Machine*, I set myself a crazy goal of appearing on 100 podcasts in a year to promote it. My group coaching platform, the One Percent Club, was in its infancy and I needed to create a new website for it, which also meant tens of thousands of words of content needed to be written (also by me), as well as almost daily calls with my web designer to approve any changes.

I'd promised our One Percenters new content every month too, including three, 90-minute live coaching sessions (with me), a weekly email (from me) containing a potential 1% improvement for their business, and an hour-long Masterclass (also by me) – a deep dive into a particular topic or strategy which would improve their business. Each 60-minute Masterclass actually took me three hours to prepare for (complete with slides, notes, and my very best jokes), and another hour to record.

There were also monthly board meetings for angel investments and masterminds to attend. I was being told off by my PR people for not being active enough on social media, so I had to become a prolific poster and feed the algorithm.

Meanwhile, I was also home-schooling my two kids (both of whom have special educational needs), my wife was signed off work with depression and anxiety, my mum had been diagnosed with dementia and my dad had a suspected heart attack.

Oh, and I had a cold.

Please pause for a moment to remember I am the chief advocate of the "ambitious lifestyle business". The irony!

With all this bubbling under the surface – and Jason unwilling to just accept my reasoning – I reached boiling point.

"I'm sorry, I can't do this anymore!"

At that moment, every single plate I had been spinning came crashing to the floor. My battery was drained. A non-stop day of back-to-back meetings, constant demands on my time and a cold was all it took for me to reach a breaking point. I simply didn't have the energy to fight. So, I lost my shit, threw my toys out of the pram, and stormed out.

What did all those smashed plates have in common? That's right – me. I'd become a bottleneck. Nothing happened without me. I wanted to run my businesses my way. My ideal job description is: "What I want, when I want, where I want, how I want... *if* I want!"

As a result, everyone was afraid to do anything without checking if it was what I wanted.

After my outburst, I spent some time working out what I *actually* wanted my life and my businesses to look like. And I realised that I needed to let go. I needed to subtract. I'd taken on too much and said "yes" too often. I'd designed a business that was far too complex and entirely reliant on me.

So I made a grovelling apology to Jason for snapping at him and suggested that rather than adding more plates to spin, or more balls to juggle, we actually try subtracting for a change.

We immediately closed down two businesses and began the process of exiting some of our long-term investments. Overnight, I made "no" my default answer:

"Can we meet for a quick coffee?" No.

"Have you got five minutes?" No.

"Do you want to check this email before I send it, boss?" No.

Each "no" was another item subtracted from the ever-growing, monstrous to-do list nagging at my brain 24/7. Top of my list of things to subtract, though, was something I'd tried (and failed) to do many times before – exit my business.

Hopefully, the fact that you're reading this book means that you're not going to be part of the "do nothing and hope for the best" brigade, so let's move on to the final option and the main topic of this book – a False EXIT.

3. THE FALSE EXIT

"Find someone better than yourself to run the business on a day-to-day basis. Remove yourself, maybe even from the building, and certainly from the nitty-gritty,"

– Sir Richard Branson

Just to recap, a False EXIT sees you, the business owner, removed from the front line – away from the day-to-day operations. But while you are no longer running the business, you do remain its owner and instead spend your time optimising it. You are the chief architect of your business.

A False EXIT comes with no lump sum pay out, there's no sailing off into the sunset and there's no guarantee your golden goose will continue to furnish you with shiny golden eggs on a regular basis. But there's also no capital gains tax bill, no brokers or lawyers to pay, no due diligence, and no immediate termination of your income. With the right strategy, processes and team in place, your business could actually continue to grow – or start growing – without needing you as an essential cog in the machine.

If you want to, you can choose to work on the business – building pipelines rather than carrying buckets – adding value to the balance sheet and helping to protect that future supply of golden eggs. But because you're no longer the godlike genius through which everything must flow, the business won't grind to a halt without you and you'll have the energy, headspace and time to realise your business's full potential, giving you purpose and a reason to get out of bed in the morning.

Decisions, Decisions

A few years ago, I was considering how to exit my info marketing business. I wasn't sure which path to take, so to help me decide, I listed the pros and cons for each of the five options:

Full Exit pros	**Full Exit cons**
• I'd get a tasty lump sum. • The business is very attractive to our target buyer. • There's zero risk to me if the business subsequently fails. • It would free up my time to work on what I love – writing books. • Post-sale, my income could be made more tax efficient, meaning I wouldn't need to work as hard. • I would no longer have to endure parts of the business I don't enjoy.	• I'd lose a steady income and need to replace it within a couple of years. • I don't actually *need* a big lump sum now. It would just feed my ego further! • I'd have to spend almost a year finding and wooing buyers, rather than growing the business. • Due diligence – urgh! • My team could lose their jobs. • Trust. I don't know the buyers and they don't know me. • The buyers might want me to "earn out". • They might want to pay in instalments, depending on their future success running my business, something that once I sell is out of my control.

Partial Exit pros	Partial Exit cons
• Err, none! You could make the "get a slice of a bigger cake" argument by bringing in an investor to help scale the business, but my desire for control and autonomy puts paid to this option.	• I immediately discounted a partial exit, because that option gave me the same downsides from the other options, with no upside.

Management Buy Out pros	Management Buy Out cons
• The team already know how to run the business. • I don't need to spend any time finding and wooing potential buyers. • The team all get to keep their jobs. • It's quite a tax efficient way of selling. • I can trust them and they can trust me. • In theory, employee productivity should go through the roof once they're owners too.	• Do they have the money? • They might not want to be owners. • If there's "owner finance", there is risk of the company failing in the future and me not getting paid. If the finance is secured against the company, the risk of failure is even higher.

Do Nothing pros	Do Nothing cons
• I get to keep a steady income. The business is designed to deliver me a very nice lifestyle. • I can continue to grow the business, achieving a higher return on investment than I could from my own "passive" investments. • Nothing changes.	• Nothing changes. Yes, I listed this as a pro *and* a con. • The business could fail in the future and I would have missed the chance to cash in my chips. • I'll keep getting "pulled back in", and won't be able to write more books. • The business will suffer from a lack of my attention while I am writing books.

And last, but not least.

False EXIT pros	False EXIT cons
• I could pick and choose when and how I work in the business (designing the machine, building pipelines, and creating new evergreen marketing campaigns – the work I love doing). • I wouldn't need to get involved with day-to-day operations, but instead just "grease the wheels", ensuring the key processes are followed.	• In the past, whenever I've not been "in" the business for a prolonged period of time, the business has always suffered. • It's possible that I might keep getting "pulled back in" and wouldn't be able to focus on writing books. • The business could still fail. • If it does fail, I've lost my chance of a significant payday.

False EXIT pros	False EXIT cons
• I can create the capacity to write more books. • I wouldn't lose any income and could still grow the business. • I have identified a trusted lieutenant within the team who I can rely on to run the day-to-day operations. • I can remain on hand to help prevent future business failure. • I can set up evergreen assets and pipeline systems to replace me. • I will have optimised the business to be firing on all cylinders before I step away. • The business could be completely systematised day-to-day, and I will still be on hand to ensure the flywheel keeps turning, as well as being available to deal with unpredictable, potentially catastrophic "black swan" events.	• Can I really let go and trust the team to do things the *right* way (i.e. the way *I* would do them)?

An admission. While completing the lists of pros and cons was useful in many ways, I was still none the wiser. Sure, I'd captured all my thoughts – everything I was worried about and all the things I hoped each option could bring me. But, unfortunately, with the exception of the Partial Exit, which could be discounted as a viable option, each possible pathway remaining had valid points in both the "for" and "against" columns.

Some of those points were more important than others, however. So, rather than relying on a five-bar gate to decide the future of my company, I chose to rank each argument on a scale of one to ten in order of importance or value to me.

Receiving a lump sum for a Full Exit scored a maximum 10 points. But then, over in the "cons" column, the fact that I didn't need a lump sum took away 8 of them. The tax efficiency of selling to the team added 6 points to the "for" column, while the fact that they didn't have the money, might not want to be owners, and the potential for "decision by committee" notched up 26 points "against" this option.

This weighted pros and cons list gave the following scores on the doors:

Full Exit

- 48 points for.
- 52 points against.
- 52% preference "against".

Management Buy Out

- 44 points for.
- 36 points against.
- 55% preference "for".

Do Nothing

- 40 points for.
- 36 points against.
- 53% preference "for".

False EXIT

- 64 points for.
- 47 points against.
- 58% preference "for".

You'll note the scores indicated a *slight* preference for a False EXIT. But it's all very close – Management Buy Out scores only 3% less, for example – and making such a big call on a preference of just above 50% is akin to putting my future in the hands of the toss of a coin. That's certainly not a mandate for making a life-changing decision – unless you're a Batman villain.

So I revisited my scores, this time looking purely at the pros and cons I had ranked as 10 out of 10 the first time around. These were the outcomes that really mattered to me but operating on a ten-point scale didn't give them enough weight. But if I shifted to a scale of 1 to 100, some of those 10s may nudge up to a 30 or 40, while others would be in the 80s or 90s. And a few (I'm looking at you due diligence) would be absolute 100-point deal-breakers.

Adding this extra weight made things much clearer:

Full Exit

- 78 points for.
- 112 points against.
- 59% preference "against".

Management Buy Out

- 60 points for.
- 81 points against.
- 57% preference "against".

Do Nothing

- 80 points for.
- 86 points against.
- 52% preference "against".

False EXIT

- 179 points for.
- 71 points against.
- 72% preference "for".

Above 70%, now that's a majority I can work with. Once I had given disproportionate weight to the outcomes that matter disproportionately, I had a clear mandate for the best option for me. I could see what truly mattered to me.

I don't need a massive payday. Keeping the business allows me to maintain my current lifestyle and fund my "get rich slowly" investment plan (as detailed in *Routine Machine*). Sure, there is a risk the business will fail but remaining involved minimises that risk. Best of all, I get to avoid the pain of due diligence, potential earn-outs, and having to replace the income having killed the golden goose.

A False EXIT enables me to give the company great value by creating systems, processes, evergreen marketing assets, and coaching the team, all while freeing me up to work on my passions – writing for and coaching ambitious, lifestyle business owners.

If you're unsure which type of exit is right for you, I'd encourage you to do the weighted pros/cons exercise. I'll include a blank template for you in the resources at the end of the book.

Which exit should you take? Which exit will you take?

If you're leaning towards a False EXIT, then I've got good news and bad news. The bad news? A False EXIT isn't a quick fix. From "I can't do this anymore!" to actually not doing this anymore took me 18 months. And those were 18 long months of hard work – planning, creating systems, training, and preparing. It took many wrong turns, dead-ends and sleepless nights before I achieved it. But I did it. I stopped carrying buckets and built my pipeline.

And that's the good news – you get to start building your pipeline, right now.

4. VISION AND VALUES

> *"It's not hard to make decisions once you know what your values are,"*
>
> – *Roy Disney*

If you intend to step back from the day-to-day running of your business but still want it to operate as if you were there then you need to ensure your people buy into your vision and values – as well as systems, frameworks, processes, etc – wholesale.

That's a big task in itself and one we'll cover as we continue. But the first – and most important – thing to consider is whether *you* are clear on your visions and values. I'm not talking about a "Live, Laugh, Love" poster on the wall, but real beliefs, morals, the way you conduct yourself, how you think people should act, what you do for people and how you want to be seen – and remembered – by others.

Because if you're not crystal clear on your vision and values, how do you expect anyone in your business to do things "your way"?

GIMME, GIMME GIMME...ONE VISION!

Why does your business exist? Could you justify your company's very existence on this planet in answering this question?

Many years ago, I was part of a mastermind group which read Simon Sinek's classic book *Start With Why*, in which he proclaims: "People don't buy what you do; they buy why you do it. And what you do simply proves what you believe."

Around the table, my fellow masterminders were all nodding sagely, while comparing themselves to Steve Jobs and Bill Gates – proper visionary leaders, who made a huge dent in the universe.

"What about you, John?" asked the host. "Why does your business exist?"

I struggled to come up with a single reason that didn't sound completely self-serving. I started my business so I could leave a day job I hated. From then on, it was about making money – to pay the bills and avoid having to return to said day job with my tail between my legs. Eventually, as I had more success, the raison d'être for my business evolved to focus on sustaining my lifestyle – to continue to provide for me and my family.

That was all that mattered to me. I didn't want to change the world. I had no desire to disrupt an industry or to revolutionise a sector. I was content to let others do that while I spent time with my kids. My peers around the mastermind table weren't letting me off though, and kept firing questions at me:

"But what about your clients, John? Why do they care that your business exists?"

I told them I didn't know; that I worked in the sports betting sector providing horse racing tips and that our members are happy when the tips win and moan when they don't. I explained that they tend to win more often than they lose, so I'm sure the members would miss the business if it disappeared overnight, but I was hardly changing the world.

But they persisted. "What problem do you solve for your clients, John?"

"I help them win more money, I suppose. Or at worst, I'm able to stop them from placing stupid bets and losing money."

"Do you follow the tips yourself?" they asked.

"Yeah, of course. I couldn't ask members to do something I'm not willing to do myself."

"How do you find the tips?" (No one expects the Spanish inquisition, right?).

"We use horse racing form data and mathematical algorithms to calculate mis-matched prices – where it's possible to back a 2/1 shot at 3/1," I told them.

"Does everyone have access to this data and algorithms?"

"No. Traditionally, only professional gamblers have had access to it. We're putting it in the hands of everyday punters."

"So anyone at all could make money following your tips?"

"Technically, yes. But most people don't have the right mindset. Most people are short term, emotional thinkers, when our most successful members are long-term, analytical thinkers."

"What if one of your clients has a gambling addiction?"

"Well, if any of our members display the symptoms of a problem, we'll refuse to work with them and encourage them to get professional help instead."

A hush descended over the room.

"So," the host concluded, "your business exists to help everyday punters make better betting decisions."

I chewed this over for a few seconds. "Yes. You're right. That's exactly what we do. A 'better decision' is unique to each person. For some, that's advice over staking plans and betting banks. For others, it's helping them find the right strategy or statistical edge. If we believe a member has a gambling problem, a 'better decision' for them is to not bet. My business exists to help everyday punters make better betting decisions!"

It took me a long time (and a lot of work) to uncover my own vision. If, like me, your vision doesn't extend much beyond "paying the bills" and "funding my lifestyle", then what will happen when you exit your business? No one else is going to care as much about your business as you do. But at least give them a fighting chance; give them a cause to rally around. You must justify the business's very existence beyond providing for you. You can't expect people to give your business everything they've got if the company's vision is simply to make *you* richer.

Let's look again at that Simon Sinek quote:

> *"People don't buy what you do; they buy why you do it. And what you do simply proves what you believe."*

Most business owners have heard the first sentence – "people don't buy what you do; they buy why you do it" many times. But when my mastermind group grilled me on the second half of the quote – "what you do simply proves what you believe" – that's when I truly discovered why my business existed. When you start a business, you get to make your own little universe in which you create all the laws. I started my business for purely selfish reasons – to earn enough money to quit the day job from hell.

But, without realising it, my vision evolved. Once the bills were covered and my family was provided for, I started to think more about the kind of work I loved to do and the people I wanted to work with. I thought about *who* I could help and *how* I could help them. I didn't consciously update my vision, though, so when I was asked, "Why does your business exist?", I gave an outdated answer: "To make money so I don't have to get a 'real job' again."

But the true reason was: "To provide me with a job I love, helping everyday punters make better betting decisions."

I had learned my lesson, and so my group coaching business was designed with a crystal-clear vision from day one.

Jason and I designed everything to scratch our own itch, to create the kind of community *we* wanted to be a part of, and to do small business coaching the way *we* wanted to, rather than "for the money" (as most "gurus" do). Sure, we could make a swimming pool full of cash selling Cayman Island Masterminds, £1,997 courses or a constant upsell "escalation model", designed purely to extract as much profit as possible from each business owner, but… urgh! (Sorry, I was just sick in my mouth for a moment).

The One Percent Club launched with six people around my kitchen table and our vision set in stone. Why does the One Percent Club exist? To help ambitious, lifestyle business owners improve their business *and* their lifestyle by 1% each week. We don't work with VC-backed startups looking to make a £10million exit. We work with ambitious, lifestyle business owners – entrepreneurs with drive and ambition, but more than anything a burning desire for a great lifestyle.

We're not here to 10x businesses. Sure, we've started dozens of businesses from scratch and scaled them to great heights. But our superpower is improving businesses. Making them marginally better every single week. And what's the point in a better business if it doesn't lead to a better life? We want to make small business owners' lives better – that's our vision. That's our why. That's what we believe, to our core. So that's what we do. And of course, as Simon Sinek reminds us, what you do proves what you believe – yet people don't buy what you do; they buy why you do it.

Why does your business exist?

"IT'S WHAT HE WOULD HAVE WANTED..."

You may remember I mentioned Guy Singh-Watson earlier. He sold his business Riverford Organic Farms to an employee-owned trust, an option that was attractive to Guy thanks to its ability to protect the vision and values upon which Riverford was built.

To accurately document his vision and values, Guy spent the best part of a year working with the Riverford team to create a "Founder's Wishes" statement, then tasked a group of trustees (initially Guy, two Riverford staff members, and two external people) to uphold the vision contained within the statement.

This wasn't a box-ticking exercise. Guy's Founder's Wishes statement was a legal document in the employee ownership sale and will be upheld for years to come, ensuring the company's actions remain consistent with their professed values and Guy's vision, the three central areas of which were:

1. Giving a fair deal to staff, suppliers, customers, and the planet.
2. A commitment to organic and to Riverford's farming roots.
3. Long-term relationships of trust with growers.

The opening line of Guy's Founder's Wishes statement tackles the question I posed to you earlier in this chapter: why does your business exist?

> *"Why we exist:*
>
> *To grow and supply the best organic food.*
>
> *As part of an independent, challenging and commercially successful business.*
>
> *Which balances the needs of customers, suppliers, the environment, and wider society.*
>
> *And provides fair and rewarding employment to our staff."*

In those few short sentences, Guy shares his vision for Riverford now and for the future. He goes into far more detail (the full Founder's Wishes statement is almost 2,000 words – I'll include a copy in the resources section), detailing how Guy's overarching vision should be executed through a set of guiding values.

Guy backed this up when announcing he was selling his remaining shares, when he said: "I will continue to use my waning energy to support the business and the values it espouses, so don't expect me to go silent."

Once you are crystal clear on your business's reason for existence, the next step is making sure everyone else knows your vision. You can do this by creating your own Founder's Wishes document.

Consider this your Declaration of Independence – designed to outlive you, ensuring your vision is honoured, long after your departure. When the founding fathers of the United States of America crafted the Declaration of Independence, they didn't focus on short-term strategy or tactics such as "who will be President?". Instead, they captured their vision, including a democratically elected President, then created frameworks and systems that would outlive them and continue to deliver their vision for the country they intended.

What's your vision? What sort of business do you want to create? What do you want to be remembered for? How do you want people to talk about you behind your back (or after you've exited)? How do you want your business to behave when you're not there?

Go Ape founders Tristram and Rebecca Mayhew created a similar Founder's Wishes statement in 2021, detailing their ambitions for the outdoor adventure company, based on the core values that shaped the company's first 20 years. From the very first site in Thetford Forest, Norfolk, the Mayhews wanted to build a company to be proud of, based on clearly defined vision and values. These were captured in writing from the very beginning, becoming Go Ape's moral compass, guiding all decisions.

So why does Go Ape exist?

> *"Go Ape's mission is to create adventures and encourage everyone to live life more adventurously. To be the best adventure company on the planet (where you can be home in time for tea)."*

So Go Ape wants "everyone to live life more adventurously", while Riverford aims to grow "the best organic food". On their own, however, such bold visions mean nothing. We can all say we want to be the best, the biggest, the most successful. We can paint our vision on the walls, but it all counts for nothing if that vision isn't lived and breathed by *everyone* in the business. It's the people on the front line who will honour (or ignore) the founder's wishes in their everyday actions.

In 1962, President John F Kennedy visited the NASA Space Center in Florida. Spotting a janitor carrying a broom, JFK ventured over to the man and asked what he was doing. The janitor's reply? "I'm helping put a man on the moon, Mr President."

Your vision doesn't have to be a moon shot, but it does need to be bold, it does need to be something that everyone can get behind, and it does need backing up with some substance – and this is what we'll look at next.

WWJD?

The foundations of your pipeline – through which every aspect of your business will flow – are your vision and values. If your vision is the Declaration of Independence, then your values are the Constitution – a set of guiding principles that uphold your vision on a daily basis.

Again, I'm not talking about some cliched core values that you paint on the walls, then ignore. I'm talking about sculpting your business in your mould, where your company shares the same vision and values that you do. Values that you *and* your business live and breathe. Values which help make every decision easier.

You can't clone yourself, but you can replicate your values. You can hire (and inspire) your team by sharing your vision. You can train and coach them using your values. You can lead based on values, educating and inspiring through them. Every process in your operations manual should align with your vision and values, and everything you do should be congruent with them.

Everything comes back to your vision and values. If you're going to put down those buckets, you'll need your team to think, act and behave like you, so you'd better make damn sure they know how.

If you're not there to carry the buckets, then everyone on your team needs to be able to answer this question before they pick up a single bucket: What would [INSERT YOUR NAME HERE] do?

If one of my team isn't sure how much to charge for a particular service, whether to refund a customer or how to respond to an unusual request, they need to be able to answer the question: What would John do? If their answer doesn't match mine, then my business isn't going to be run the way I want, and I'm likely to either get frustrated with my team, disillusioned with my business or – worse – start carrying buckets myself again.

How do my team know what I would do? It's simple, really. They know my vision and my values. They know them inside out. I've spent years repeating them, parrot-fashion. I mention my core values so often, they almost feel like catchphrases.

If one of my team approaches me with a question they can't answer, I often have to bite my tongue. Why? Because I know the answer and *could* give them the solution in about five seconds flat. But if I keep feeding them the answers without showing my workings, they'll keep asking me every time they have a question, so I need to build a pipeline that removes me as the bottleneck.

Next time you're asked a question, use the opportunity to explain how you reached the solution and, crucially, link it either to your vision for the business or one of your core values.

I own a couple of businesses and they all share very similar core values because they're *my* core values. It's far easier to have company values that are truly aligned with your own, rather than fashionable statements to try and curry favour with your clients.

Don't *choose* core values; *have* core values. Instead of asking "What *should* we value?", ask yourself "What *do* we value?". What do you believe deep to your core? What values are as natural as breathing to you? What beliefs do you have that you would still maintain even if they were a disadvantage, unfashionable or made you unpopular?

"I love cigarettes. It's one of the things that makes life really worth living." Those were the words of Ross Millhiser, who marketed cigarettes to women and young people in the 1950s and 60s. If Millhiser were to make those comments today, he would be cancelled – publicly shamed and forced to apologise and/or resign. I don't share Millhiser's values, but they prove my point. He truly believed in them to his core. And they are *his* values, not what he thinks the market wants to hear or what will make him look good.

I would go as far as to say that some people should disagree with your values. They may poke fun at them, strongly believe the polar opposite or question why on earth you believe in them. That's when you know you've got true values – when you will defend them to the bitter end because they're in your core. You haven't just copied someone else's or chosen cliched statements that will make you look smart.

Start by writing down everything you value. Don't rule anything out at the beginning, just brain dump all the things that you believe you hold dear. However, only a few values can truly be core. If you've got 15 core values, then you've got no core values. Three to six seems to be the sweet spot, so ask yourself some tough questions to eliminate some of the weaker beliefs and discover what's true to your core:

1. What values do you hold so fundamentally that you would defend them, regardless of whether they were popular or not?
2. If you won the lottery this weekend and never needed to work again, would you still live by these values?
3. Can you see yourself continuing to treat these values as sacred ten years from now?
4. How about 25 years or 100?
5. Would you encourage your grandchildren and great-grandchildren to also live by them?

My core values are fun, trustworthiness and community. These three values pass the tough questions test, so I know they go deep. I need to ensure they go to the core of my business, too. When someone joins my info-marketing team, I share my founder's vision with them: we exist to help everyday people live better lives through the power of knowledge and information. For my coaching business, we exist to help ambitious, lifestyle business owners improve their business and lifestyle, by 1% each week.

Knowing why the company exists helps answer a lot of the "what would John do?" questions. When they have a decision to make, they can ask themselves: which solution helps everyday people live better lives through knowledge and information? Or, which option helps more ambitious, lifestyle business owners to stack up a 1% win?

Once my team embodies the founder's vision, we do the same for core values. I explain in great detail, and using an abundance of stories and examples, why those values are important and how to execute on them:

1. Fun: I want to enjoy coming to work, not take myself too seriously, and achieve great things with a smile on my face. I also want my team and my clients to be having fun too. We do some things just because they're fun, even if they're illogical or lose money.
2. Trustworthiness: I work in sectors where there are no end of charlatans, snake-oil salesmen and downright con artists. So it's essential that my word (and my company's word) is my bond. We do the right thing – every time.
3. Community: I don't just want to build businesses. I want to build tribes. I want to build supportive communities, where tribe members feel "this is my place – full of my people!" We value relationships over transactions.

I can't underestimate just how much time I spend reinforcing these values with my team. Every time I answer a question, every story I tell, I refer back to one of those three values in some way. When a team member spots that a client has been billed twice (but hasn't complained), I don't just tell them to process the refund. Instead I ask: "How can we demonstrate our trustworthiness here?" And the decision becomes simple. We do the right thing, every time.

When they ask for a small budget to run a competition for members, I simply ask: "Will it be fun? Will it help build the community?" Again, the question answers itself. We do some things just because they're fun: relationships over transactions.

THE ACE OF CLUBS

In 1996, Exeter Rugby Club were a fourth-division backwater team. Captained by lock Rob Baxter, the club embraced the sport's evolution into the professional era, rebranding as Exeter Chiefs in 1999, and slowly climbing up the leagues. They eventually established themselves as a second-tier stalwart, spending a decade in the Championship without threatening the top-flight.

After his playing career ended in 2009, Baxter became the Chiefs' Director of Rugby and oversaw a step-change in the club's fortunes – taking them into the Premiership for the first time in their history, keeping them there against all odds, and winning their first domestic silverware – the LV= Cup in 2014. More success followed, with Baxter managing to attract top internationals to the club's newly developed Sandy Park home, as well as nurturing outstanding homegrown talent.

The Chiefs finished runners-up in the Premiership in 2015/16 and were never out of the top two in the next six seasons, winning the Premiership twice in that time as well as two Anglo-Welsh Cups and becoming champions of Europe in 2020.

This is the equivalent of my football team, little old Plymouth Argyle, winning the Premier League, FA Cup and Champions League in the next few years. Now I'm the most green-tinted optimist, but even I can't see that happening any time soon.

So how did Rob Baxter do it? How did he turn a bunch of lower-league players from a rugby backwater into not just the best team in the country, but the best in Europe?

He did it by installing a key set of core values, chosen by the team itself, and truly lived and breathed, as Baxter himself explains:

> *"I created a questionnaire: tell me the three or four of the most important things you want other people to see in our team and the things you want to have in our team itself.*

When there's 40 or 50 people each telling you three or four things, you come up with quite a big list of words. There were a lot of rugby words: relentless; dominant; combative; physical; fast; all that kind of stuff. But then there's also an emotional level of words that come out. The word enjoyment came out three or four times with players being emotional or showing we care.

I put all the words that came back into three categories. And that's where ACE came from.

Attitude is your mental approach to the game. How are you gonna approach it? What are the qualities you're gonna show, mentally and emotionally that people see?

Commitment is about your preparation. What's your commitment to getting physically prepared? How hard are you gonna work? Are you gonna be on time? Are you gonna maximise your weight sessions? Are you gonna maximise your running sessions? Are you gonna eat and sleep, do the right things?

And then the third one, Enjoyment – how are we gonna feel about what we're doing?

It was empowered by the players and the elements they wanted. Those three categories (Attitude, Commitment, Enjoyment) have really been the backbone of nearly everything we've done."

Could you ask your team to come up with a few words to describe the vision they have and the values by which they want to live (and work)? This, I feel, was a crucial factor in the Chiefs' success. The core values weren't dictated to from above, they were chosen together as a team.

The Chiefs' values weren't just painted on the walls of Sandy Park as window dressing, box ticking or for show, they were there as a constant reminder: This is who we are. This is who we want to be. This is how we show up – every day.

If I ask someone who knows you well, they should be able to tell me your core values without seeing them on a wall – they'll know them from your daily actions. Remember, what you do simply proves what you believe.

I recently visited some secondary schools to choose where my daughter will spend her teenage years. One school we visited spoke passionately about their "whole child" values, something which, yes, was painted on the walls, but which we also saw demonstrated by every teacher we spoke with, each pupil we met, and all communications with the school.

By contrast, another school listed their core values as: "Teaching and Learning; Leadership; Community; Learning Environment and The Person." Not one of these values shone through from my visit. In fact, the only core value I saw lived and breathed was discipline – it was a very quiet school, full of well-behaved, well-dressed children going quietly about their work.

Please don't paint clichéd core values that sound good on your walls – instead choose values you truly live by or aspire to live by. Those values should be specific to you and maybe up for debate.

If Exeter Chiefs' core values had been decided by senior management, would "enjoyment" have been one of them? I highly doubt it. But for the team themselves – the guys who turn up for training every day, push their bodies to the absolute limit, and give their all on the pitch – it's vital they enjoy their job and be able to work with a smile on their face, even if (maybe especially if) the pressure is intense, with silverware or titles on the line.

Within a high-pressure environment, you could argue whether enjoyment as a core value works or not (the Chiefs' trophy room would suggest it does). But that's exactly my point. You should be able to debate the validity of your values with someone who has different values to you.

Amazon boss Jeff Bezos has made low prices and excellent customer service key values in his business. Michael O'Leary at Ryanair would agree wholeheartedly with the low prices ethos, but I can imagine a heated debate between the two CEOs about whether "the customer is always right". Add Bernard Arnault, chairman of Louis Vuitton Moët Hennessy, into the discussion and he'd rail against low prices.

Consider the clichéd values painted on the wall of that secondary school I visited with my daughter. Could you really debate their core values? Could you make the case that a school shouldn't value teaching or learning?

Now look again at my core values – fun, trustworthiness, and community. You could easily argue against all three. If you're a funeral director, I wouldn't imagine putting the fun in funerals would be your priority. Trustworthiness gives me an advantage only because I work in sectors where trust is a rare commodity. And while my businesses thrive on building tribes around a common goal, that could actually hurt a business that relies on confidentiality.

MY GREENGROCER WON'T SELL ME BLUEBERRIES

I love blueberries. That's why I've got an automatically recurring blueberry subscription with Riverford Organic Farms ensuring my overnight oats, pancakes and waffles always have some nice plump, juicy blueberries to accompany them.

Or at least they did until I received the following email:

> *"Dear John,*
>
> *We hope you've been enjoying our blueberries as much as we have – but sadly, the season has come to an end. Because you had blueberries in your future order, we wanted to let you know that they'll be removed from deliveries from Monday 3rd October.*
>
> *You may find blueberries in the supermarket all year round, but they will have travelled a long way, or been grown under heated glass, at huge environmental cost. That's why we celebrate what's in season, and only stock produce that stays under our carbon emission limits."*

Now, I'd happily eat blueberries all year round. I'm sure Riverford could find a supply of blueberries throughout the winter. After all, their job is to sell fruit and veg, right? They could make a lot more money by selling products out of season. However, that would go against their core values – the values that they live and breathe.

The reason Riverford won't sell me blueberries in the winter is the same reason they've planted 800 trees this year, reduced their paper packaging by 60%, and swapped all their plastic bags to be fully compostable. It's why they're committed to 100% of their delivery fleet using electric vehicles, why they'll never transport fruit or veg by air, and how they make tough decisions to arrive at the best (or least harmful) option.

It's also why they've been voted as one of the top 100 companies to work for, with feedback such as, "This organisation is run on strong values/principles", and with team members declaring, "I feel proud to work for this organisation".

We got to know Guy Singh-Watson's Founder's Wishes for Riverford earlier – to grow and supply the best organic food, as part of an independent, challenging and commercially successful business, which balances the needs of customers, suppliers, the environment, and wider society, and provides fair and rewarding employment to its staff.

That's a lot to remember. But, just like Rob Baxter's ACE framework at Exeter Chiefs, Guy has distilled those Riverford values into three categories:

> *"We have three guiding values, summed up in five words: WE – DO IT – OUR WAY."*

Those five words are broken down thus:

- WE: Demonstrates that the business is a collective effort. That no one is in it for themselves, and that everyone has a voice, as well as a responsibility. That knowledge is best shared, and established practices are there to be questioned – by anyone. The group decides what's best for the group. Mistakes are encouraged, rules are minimised and milestones are celebrated.
- DO IT: The importance of doing things well, right down to the fine detail. Sharing knowledge and enthusiasm – especially about food, vegetables, and farming – is an essential part of the business, as is having a commercially viable business model. It's made clear that what they don't do (not selling me blueberries in winter, for instance) is as important as what they do do.
- OUR WAY: Guy says: "We will make our own decisions, based on our own knowledge, analysis and values and, where necessary, have the confidence to follow a different path – to do things our way." This often involves contrary thinking, embracing values

such as "the customer is not always right", "market forces are not always right" and even "we are not a cult" – recognising that balancing ideological values with a commercially viable business model means not everyone will agree and that's just fine.

Three values, five words – making it easy for everyone to remember, easy for everyone to live and breathe these values, and easier to make tough decisions where the "right answer" isn't obvious.

Take the common tomato. I may not be able to bake blueberry muffins in March, but I can enjoy a nice homemade spaghetti bolognese, made with fresh, organic tomatoes from Riverford year-round. I've never given too much thought to where my tomatoes have come from before but Guy certainly has:

> *"There are two options: growing out-of-season produce at home using artificial heat (generated by burning gas or oil), or importation. In the Riverford Sustainable Development Project, Exeter University concluded that importation by road is by far the greener choice.*
>
> *For every kilo of tomatoes grown in a UK hothouse, 2-3 kilos of C02 are released into the atmosphere. When we can't grow tomatoes at home without heat, we truck over naturally sun-ripened ones from Spain. Growing tomatoes in the UK with artificial heat would produce anywhere from two to ten times as much carbon – and sun-ripened toms taste better, too."*

Notice what Guy is actually doing here, both with his data-driven sun-ripened-tomatoes example, and his simple (but detailed) WE – DO IT – OUR WAY vision. As with Rob Baxter's ACE framework, both give their team something infinitely more powerful than "the right answer". They've handed over their entire decision-making framework. Any member of their team, whether they're a flanker or a farmer, a scrum half or a veg scrubber, can make values-based decisions on a daily basis easily without needing to ask the boss.

So, should they sell blueberries in the winter? You tell me…

EAT SLEEP VALUES REPEAT

Jack Welch, widely acknowledged as the greatest CEO of the 20th century, always carried a small, laminated card showing his vision and values for General Electric:

> *"Find a Better Way Every Day. Have a passion for excellence, hate bureaucracy and all the nonsense that comes with it."*

Jack Welch understood that vision and values that are out of sight are out of mind.

My team makes fun of me because barely a meeting goes by without me parroting one or more of our core values or hammering home the vision once again. The way I see it, though, is unless your team is mocking you, you haven't repeated your message anywhere near often enough. I want my vision and values to be top of mind at all times for my team. I'd like to think that if I asked any one of my team to articulate our company's vision, and the core values that underpin it, they'd be able to recite it without hesitation.

This is the result of my constant repetition. Because it's repeated, it's reinforced. Because it's reinforced, it's truly lived and breathed. My team develops muscle memory and, as a result, lives and breathes our core values, making working towards our vision second nature. You can't just write a Founder's Wishes statement, file it away in a drawer and expect people to abide by it.

Former Johnson & Johnson CEO Jim Burke estimated that he spent 40% of his time communicating the company "credo" – a Founder's

Wishes statement created by Robert Wood Johnson in 1943 that remains largely unaltered to this day. Very few CEOs spend almost half of their working lives devoted to honouring the company's vision and values, especially when those values are almost 100 years old.

But as Johnson & Johnson proudly declare: "Our credo is more than just a moral compass. We believe it's a recipe for business success. The fact that Johnson & Johnson is one of only a handful of companies that have flourished through more than a century of change is proof of that."

A century of change, but with consistent vision and values reinforced and repeated again and again from the very top.

How did Ray Kroc ensure his vision and values were adhered to with more than 7,500 McDonald's franchises? Repetition. "If I had a brick for every time I've repeated the phrase Q, S, C, and V (quality, service, cleanliness and value)," says Kroc, "I think I'd probably be able to bridge the Atlantic Ocean with them."

Guy Singh-Watson may not be a shareholder in Riverford Organic Farms now, but he still takes every opportunity he can to reinforce his vision and values. Every week for more than 30 years, Guy has written a personal letter to customers, a copy of which is popped into their veg boxes. I always look forward to reading Guy's missives, which are a mix of education, insights, opinion, and charm (with occasional rants thrown in for good measure).

Through this weekly repetition, I and 50,000 other recipients learn about the vision and values behind the farmer. We discover that Riverford truly are living and breathing these values.

We discover the origins for Guy's love of farming ("Since donning my first wellies, I have always wanted to be a farmer"); why doing the right thing is important ("I farm organically because it just feels right. I have a science degree, my tractors use GPS, and I wholeheartedly embrace the IT revolution. But I still find that what feels right is a good aid to making good decisions"); his hatred of supermarkets ("Supermarket buyers make second-hand car salesmen seem like priests"); or even how to source a flock of ducks to deal with a slug infestation ("I tried the paper. I tried the free ads. I even tried the internet. It is rather reassuring to have discovered that, in the end, the best place to buy a duck is in the pub"); before discovering a flaw with duck-powered pest control ("They all waddled off down to the river never to return").

Repeat, repeat, repeat.

If your people aren't mocking you for your constant repetition of your vision and values, rolling their eyes, saying, "Oh here they go again!" every time you shine a light on a particular value, then you're simply *not* repeating them often enough.

Either that or your people aren't the right people. You've got the right people, right?

5. THE RIGHT PEOPLE

"Leadership is about making others better as a result of your presence, and making sure that impact lasts in your absence,"

- Sheryl Sandberg

NO MAN IS AN ISLAND

To the nearest whole number, my dream number of employees is zero. You see, I'm not one of these inspirational, charismatic leaders. I do my best work alone, locked away in my home office, with the outside world well and truly outside.

In the beginning, there was me. Just me, alone at home knocking up websites and learning how this marketing thing worked. Then, my friend Jason joined me – initially as my first employee and, a few years later, as my business partner. We both worked from our respective homes and it worked well. Hiring Jason to do the things I didn't enjoy (or wasn't good at) freed me up to focus on the things I did enjoy and was good at.

The business continued to grow, so I hired Ryan, a web designer, who, despite living 30 miles away, also worked from home. This went well too, which led to me making a dangerous assumption: I believed that every employee I took on would further increase the company's growth. So I hired Jacob. And Liam. And Joseph, Emma, Mark, Jessie, Stuart, Laura, Lorraine, Alfie, Amelia, Chloe, and Stephen. (Some names have been changed to protect the guilty).

It no longer seemed practical to have everyone working from home, so I signed a lease on not one, but two offices. Over the course of a few months, I increased my overheads by around £300,000 a year – all underwritten and personally guaranteed by yours truly. I told myself: "It's fine. Each new member of staff multiplies our output. If I can earn six figures a year on my own in my home office then a team of 15 should easily achieve seven!"

Spoiler alert – that's not what happened. Instead, I found myself dealing with HR issues rather than growing my business. My time was no longer spent alone in my home office focused on revenue-generating tasks but in one of our new offices, surrounded by my team, focused on firefighting their issues.

"My door's always open," I told them. "Let me know if you've got any questions or need any help."

And boy, did they have questions…

> *"What colour should the button on the sales page be?"*
>
> *"How big do you think the image should be?"*
>
> *"Do you think I should send this email in Times New Roman or Helvetica?"*

And it wasn't restricted to the actual work, either:

> *"The fridge is broken."*
>
> *"The kitchen is untidy."*
>
> *"What shall I do when the toilet paper runs out?" (Really? How do these people function in the real world?)*

Before long, cracks started to form in the team. Chloe refused to work with Jacob. Joseph slept with Liam's girlfriend. Alfie spent all day chatting with friends online, while Amelia wasted hours watching Disney movies as "research" for a quick logo design.

One thing that nobody was doing, however, was generating any revenue – least of all me because my attention was constantly being dragged away from the tasks that brought in the dough to firefight personnel issues. I felt like my job title had gone from CEO and Entrepreneur to HR Rep and Agony Uncle.

I started to hate going into the office, so I avoided it. I went back to working from home most of the week, only popping into the office on a Friday afternoon. From Monday to Thursday, I was as productive as I'd ever been, able to focus on the important tasks which keep the lights on. But I'd be brought back down to earth with a bump each Friday afternoon, as I discovered the 15 people that I was paying to bring me leverage had actually achieved less than I had on my own in the previous four days.

To make matters worse, they would save up a litany of complaints and problems for me to sort, knowing the "HR guy who pays the wages" was popping in. They all wanted pay rises, an advance on their wages and next Thursday off to babysit their sick hamster. After 18 months of haemorrhaging cash, I couldn't take it anymore and, as I mentioned earlier, attempted my first exit by "retiring" aged 27 – handing over 49% of my business for free, simply to escape the monster I'd created.

When I had no choice but to return a year later, the team had naturally shrunk – many leaving to escape the toxic environment. My first task as returning CEO was to close both offices, making half of those remaining redundant, including several members of the same family. If I hadn't done so, the business would not have survived three more months, but I still felt responsible for everyone and to this day that remains my worst day in business.

Before long though, we were back to doing what had worked so well for us in the past – a small team of three, all working from home. It would be seven years before I hired anyone else. It seemed obvious that when I work alone, I thrive. The minute other people are involved, I'm nowhere near as effective because I waste so much energy managing them. My initial assumption – that hiring 15 people would mean we'd earn 15 times the revenue – was way out. At most, revenue doubled with the larger team, while overheads increased exponentially. Alone in my home office, I was making ten grand a month. With a team of 15 over two offices, we were *losing* £25k a month.

For years, I told myself: "You're better off alone, John." Then I met Joe, who showed me just how wrong I was.

Joe was a freelance content writer, who produced good work, on time, every time. We didn't have a lot of work for him, though, and just paid him piecemeal for each article he delivered.

He would constantly ask: "Do you have any vacancies? I'd love to work full time for you guys." And I'd instantly respond: "Sorry Joe. We don't employ anyone anymore." I explained how my previous experience of managing a team had scarred me for life. But Joe refused to take no for an answer. He assured me he was self-motivated and wouldn't need managing. He promised to do everything in his power to deliver a positive ROI on his wages.

His persistence began to wear me down. Eventually, I told him that I had an appointment in Birmingham the next month and if he could get himself there, we could have a face-to-face chat – but no promises jobwise. Sure enough, Joe travelled the 150 miles or so from Norwich to Birmingham at his own expense and we met at a pizza restaurant in the Bullring shopping hub. And by the time we'd worked our way through our calzones, we'd hatched a plan.

Joe became my first new employee for seven years but with a clearly defined get-out clause after six months. I'd guarantee Joe's wages for that period but beyond that, if he didn't bring in enough business to cover his wages, then we'd go back to our freelance working pattern with no hard feelings.

He started in the September and together we planned the launch of a new membership service, which was launched in October. By November, we'd sold enough memberships to cover Joe's salary and by the six-month review point, he didn't get the sack – he got a pay rise instead.

Joe was soon joined by two more superstar team members and this far-smaller team of five achieved what the rapidly assembled bunch of 15 could not – true leverage. Over the course of a few years, turnover increased ten-fold and profits shot up five-fold.

So what was the difference between the two teams? First and foremost, it was the quality of the individuals in each team. In the early years, Jason and I advertised in our local job centre, interviewed everyone who applied and hired everyone we liked. We once hired three people for one position!

For our superstar team, however, we used a specialist recruitment agency to sift through the applicants. This agency cast the net nationwide, delivering us a shortlist of the very best candidates. We carried out multiple interviews with each candidate, asking them to complete a sample piece of work – nothing too taxing, but something to demonstrate how they would approach the role in real life.

For example, when hiring a copywriter, we asked candidates to condense 350 words of text into 100 words or less. This demonstrated each candidate's process for deciding what's important and what's not. We can see how ruthless they are and whether the abbreviated work still reads well.

One candidate immediately failed the test (and missed out on the job) before he even opened his mouth in the interview. This was because when he handed in his work, I could see he'd filled both sides of an A4 sheet of paper. Instead of condensing the word count to 100 or less, he'd expanded it closer to a thousand. They may have been the greatest thousand words ever written, but they were also a perfect demonstration of an inability to follow simple instructions – a massive red flag when I'm hiring people to work autonomously and remotely.

Aside from hiring superstars via a strict deselection process, we also kept overheads to a minimum. Once I closed both offices, they stayed shut and everyone worked from home. I kept the team small, preferring to outsource to freelancers, aided by software and systems rather than grow the overheads permanently.

My business journey looks something like this:

- First, I did everything myself.
- Then I naively thought that the more people I employed, the more my business would earn.
- When that didn't work, I refused to employ anyone.
- Finally, I found my happy place – employing a small team of the right people and supporting them with high quality systems, software, and outsourced third parties.

I still don't enjoy leading or managing people. I'm a lone wolf. I work best alone. But if I work alone, I can't exit my business. If I stop working, I stop earning. Without a team, I don't have a business. I've got a self-employed job. As *E-Myth* author Michael Gerber says: "If your business depends on you, you don't own a business—you have a job. And it's the worst job in the world because you're working for a lunatic!"

Now, I'm not here to dictate the size of your business or how many people you should employ but you're reading a book about exiting the day-to-day operations of your business and that's hard to do without replacing you with other people.

Or should I say – replacing you with the *right* people.

NO DICKHEADS ON THE BUS

In his 2001 classic *Good to Great*, Jim Collins presents his findings from a five-year study of 1,435 Fortune 500 companies in order to find the common characteristics of previously "good" businesses (on a par with the market average), who broke through to become "great" (beating the market by almost seven times, sustained for a 15-year period).

Collins' team found that a mere 11 companies met this stringent criteria and set about studying those businesses in detail. They unearthed several surprising correlations – common factors that the 11 good-to-great companies all shared, yet none of the 1,424 comparison companies did.

One of the primary correlations that Collins' team discovered was that the good-to-great companies focused on people ahead of strategy. Collins talks about this "First Who, then What" framework using the metaphor of a business being like a bus:

> *"The good-to-greats first got the right people on the bus, the wrong people off the bus and the right people in the right seats, and then they figured out where to drive it.*
>
> *The old adage, 'People are your most important asset' turns out to be wrong. If you're making something great, people are not your most important asset. The right people are."*

It's no surprise that my early attempts at building a team failed – I was focusing first on *what* my team was going to do, then looking at *who* was available. Yet when I sat down with Joe in that pizza restaurant, the *who* was nailed. Between us, we simply needed to figure out *what* we were going to do. I knew I wanted Joe on my bus. We'd choose our destination later.

If, like me, you're not very good at managing people, Collins' study comes with good news. Those 11 good-to-great companies *didn't* have better managers than the comparison companies. In many cases, their managers were mediocre. Instead, they had better people, who didn't need managing.

"The moment you feel the need to tightly manage someone," Collins says, "you've likely made a hiring mistake. The best people don't need to be managed."

Let me repeat that – the best people don't need to be managed.

When I think about the best performers I've had in my teams, they hardly needed managing at all. They've all been self-motivated, self-disciplined, and bought into the company vision. I can tell them where the bus needs to go and then relax, knowing it will arrive safely, on time, and without incident. My job is to get out of their way, enabling and equipping them to get a full day's uninterrupted work done, progressing our vision.

By contrast, I found myself micromanaging my worst performers. I'd set myself reminders for *their* tasks, proofread their emails before letting them loose on to the general public, and questioning their every move. I couldn't trust them. I *didn't* trust them. If I asked them to drive the bus, I honestly couldn't guess where it might end up, when it would get there, or what state it would be in when it did arrive. Some days it wouldn't even leave the depot.

The right people don't need managing. So, who are the right people?

I believe the right people have to share your core values. Values that are not shared, are not likely to be adhered to – and that means your business won't be run *your* way without you. Conflicting values will mean your business behaves in conflicting ways, making confusing decisions for the wrong reasons, which is a clear recipe for disaster.

Core values were another correlation found among those 11 good-to-great companies. "Core values are essential for enduring greatness," says Jim Collins. "And yet it doesn't seem to matter *what* those core values are. The point is not what core values you have, but that you *have* core values, that you *know* what they are, that you build them *explicitly* into the organisation and that you *preserve them* over time."

In other words, don't simply paint your core values on the wall – truly live and breathe them. Be so clear on your vision and values, so determined to honour them, that you refuse to allow anyone on your bus who is unwilling or unable to share them. The right people will buy into your vision, but they shouldn't buy into your values. Why not? Because they shouldn't need to "buy in" to them as they should already share them. They're *their* values too.

The right people can also be trusted. Neuroscientist Paul Zak discovered a correlation between high-performing companies and high levels of trust. Zak found that, compared to their counterparts at firms where trust was low, employees at high-trust companies reported:

- 50% higher productivity.
- 13% fewer sick days.
- 40% less burnout.
- 106% more energy at work.
- 74% less stress.

Zak also discovered that trust is reciprocated. When people demonstrate their trust in us, our brains produce oxytocin, a hormone that is linked to warm, fuzzy feelings, and known to lower stress and anxiety. This flood of oxytocin then motivates us to reciprocate – to repay the trust shown in us. If you trust people, they're more likely to be trustworthy.

Of course, we've all heard horror stories about the star salesperson stealing the client base or the business partner who changes the locks and empties the till. In his study, Zak found that around 5% of subjects were "unconditional non-reciprocators" (or "bastards" as his team nicknamed them!). Some people *are* bastards and it's very difficult to know who you can trust without the benefit of hindsight. But when you hire the right people, based on attitude rather than aptitude, you're more likely to weed out any rotten apples.

If you don't want bastards, don't hire dickheads. Originally introduced by New Zealand mental skills coach Gilbert Enoka, the "no dickheads" rule helped the All Blacks win back-to-back world cups in 2011 and 2015. The policy is policed by the players and is a crucial part of the All Blacks' selection process.

Enoka described dickheads as "people putting themselves ahead of the team, people who think they're entitled to things or expect the rules to be different for them; people operating deceitfully in the dark or being unnecessarily loud about their work. A dickhead makes everything about *them*. Often teams put up with it because a player has so much talent. We look for early warning signs and wean the big egos out pretty quickly. Our motto is, 'If you can't change the people, change the people.'"

Do you check for dickheads when interviewing new hires? Do you do any basic background checks on the *person* you're hiring as opposed to the highly polished professional who turned up for the interview? Most small business owners don't even bother to check references.

Of course, the no dickheads rule won't be a cast-iron guarantee that your new hire won't be tempted to nick your database or stick their hand in the till but it's a bloody good indicator.

The right people are also more likely to be self-starters. If you're going to put down your buckets, the last thing you want is people standing around waiting to be told what to do. Again, including a small task as part of your application process can help the right people shine through. I was recruiting for a marketing role recently and received a few hundred applications – mostly through an online job marketplace where it's really easy to apply for dozens of jobs with a few clicks. I added a small task:

> *"In order to progress to the interview stage, please send a short (500 words or less) sales letter to me. What are you selling? Yourself. You're the product. I'm the prospect. Convince me to interview you."*

Out of 300 applicants, I received just 12 sales letters. That's 96% of applicants who couldn't be bothered to do a little work in order to get an interview. What makes me think they would behave any differently if they got the job? I made a point of interviewing everyone who completed the task, even those who weren't suited to the role, because I wanted to congratulate them for being the *right people.* They weren't right for me or for this role, but for someone, somewhere, they'd be perfect.

I encouraged them to continue displaying this attitude in their job search, assuring them that they were already in the top 4% of applicants as a result. If they carry that attitude throughout their career, they'll go far.

INTRODUCING THE OH SHIT-O-METER

How do you know whether your current team consists of the right people? There's a surprisingly easy (and devastatingly effective) way to find out, with one thought exercise. One by one, work through your team, imagining the following two scenarios:

1. They've called in sick this morning.
2. They've handed in their resignation.

What's your initial gut reaction? If your very first thought isn't, "Oh shit! What are we gonna do?", that's a clear indication that the person either isn't the right person or is sitting in the wrong seat. This "Oh Shit-o-meter" exercise warns you of the perils ahead if you persevere with this person. Picture a dial from one to ten on the "Oh Shit!" scale. A reading of one means you wouldn't notice their absence (and might even welcome it), while a score of ten suggests that you'd spend most of the day running around like a headless chicken, shouting: "Oh shit! Oh shit! Oh shit!"

Run through this exercise quickly now, and note down the scores for each of your team. What does your gut tell you? In my experience, your gut isn't always right (especially when it says "everything will be fine"). But you absolutely should listen when your gut is trying to warn you of something – your inbuilt Oh Shit-o-meter is incredibly accurate at identifying the wrong people.

You should also pay attention if it gives wildly different readings for the two different scenarios.

On a scale of one to ten, you may score the first scenario (the team member calling in sick) higher on the Oh Shit-o-meter scale than the second (where they quit for good). That's a huge warning sign, that while in the short term their absence would be hugely problematic (someone's got to carry those buckets today), in the long term, their absence would actually be preferred.

If you react with a shrug of the shoulders, or even relief, then that person really isn't essential for the success of your business and you should probably consider their long-term future.

By contrast, if your Oh Shit-o-meter sounds the alarm loud and proud, then you've probably got a superstar on your hands, who you heavily rely on. They're definitely the right person and you need to ensure that you look after them.

STICK TO THE PLAN, STAN

A key skill that will enable the right people to run your business the right way (your way) in your absence is the ability to follow instructions.

The False EXIT pipework leans heavily on systems and processes, which you'll consciously design and implement before you exit. Once you've exited, you must be able to trust your team to actually follow these processes and not to "wing it" or do their own thing.

That's not to say that we want a bunch of robots working for us, forbidding them to deploy any independent thinking whatsoever. But for the majority of tasks, you will have already designed and optimised the key processes and battle-tested them in the real world. In other words, you know they work when they're followed. If your team has ideas to improve things, that should be encouraged. But it should be encouraged via a process of collating, testing, and implementing those suggestions. That process should *not* involve the team member ignoring your proven processes and doing whatever the hell they feel like.

One of my key frustrations managing people over the last few decades has been individuals thinking their gut instinct is better than the proven processes I've spent years (and my own money) battle-testing in the real world, on the front lines of my business. From the mediocre MD who thought our direct response marketing business would be better without doing direct response marketing to the technically skilled worker who point-blank refused to produce our most profitable product of all time, because he "didn't like it".

I once employed someone to improve the conversion rate on our websites. I explained that one of our values was constant, never-ending improvement, using data to upgrade every aspect of the customer journey. I handed over the results from the past few years of running these tasks myself.

And guess what? He ignored every piece of data. He thought he knew best and went with his gut. As a result, almost every change he made to our website made things measurably worse, not better. And because he didn't follow the proven processes, he also didn't track any of the changes he made so we had no way of knowing what was working and what wasn't. I employed him for constant never-ending improvement and he delivered constant, never-ending deterioration instead. But that's *my* fault.

Why? Because I managed him by abdication, not delegation. I had no metrics to measure his success (or failure). I didn't set up any red flag alerts to warn me that things were going wrong. Even when I *did* notice that things were going awry, I didn't remind him of our vision and values. I didn't signpost our decision-making framework or our proven processes. I let him do his own thing for far too long, eventually firing him for his terrible performance – but not until he'd damaged almost every aspect of my business.

The right people love to be held accountable because when you measure their success with easily quantifiable metrics, their talent becomes obvious. Your best salesperson *wants* their sales figures displayed for all to see, while your worst prefers to tell stories – "the economy's too tough", "marketing hasn't given me good leads", "the product's too expensive". If you've got someone who hides behind stories to excuse their poor performance and avoids being held to account with quantifiable metrics, it may be time to ask them to vacate the bus.

When I think about the superstars that I've worked with over the years, they all wanted to be held accountable. They liked setting targets and they loved smashing them. As if to say: "Look! Look how good I am. See what I'm capable of." By contrast, when I think of the poorest performers, they all shied away from being measured, preferring to tell tales that justify their inability to deliver. "Don't measure *me*," they'll say. "It's not *my* fault that I didn't get anywhere near my target. Personally, I think the target was wrong in the first place."

The right people also love autonomy. They don't want to be micromanaged and they aren't the sort to sit around twiddling their thumbs, awaiting instructions. No, they're go-getters. They're self-motivated. They're driven. Just tell them where the bus is going and they'll figure out the best route, and probably service the engine on the way.

Now, you may feel there's a conflicting agenda here. On the one hand, we're looking for people who don't need to be told what to do, are highly self-motivated, and able to make decisions independently. On the other hand, we want people who stick to the plan, Stan – those who won't deviate from proven processes, don't think they know better, and won't just "wing it".

This is why it's so important to hire based on your vision and values. If your people feel *real* synergy, if your company's values closely match their own, they're far more likely to buy into your overarching vision. If you can demonstrate your systems and processes have been optimised to deliver on that vision and that there's a decision-making framework to help them to make better values-based decisions, they're less likely to do their own thing.

Your systems and processes should be there as scaffolding to support the right people, to help them make the right decisions without the need for you to micromanage them. Remember, the right people don't need managing – especially if their vision and values are aligned with yours.

YOU'RE GONNA NEED A BIGGER BUS

Nobody will ever care about your business as much as you do. No one will work as hard or be as efficient as you. But, unless you're going to keep driving the bus until the day you die, you'll probably need to invite some people along for the ride. And if you're hiring to replace yourself as the glue that holds the business together, it's not out of the question to hire two or even three people.

It's not pure ego for me to say that, in general, business owners work harder than anyone else. Again and again, I see small business owners putting in 100-hour weeks (or more), working through weekends and holidays, while paying themselves minimum wage (or worse) for the privilege.

Remember my restaurant-owning friend, working an 80-hour week for 12 grand a year? He's the rule, not the exception. Exiting him from his business would require a new head barman, front of house manager, kitchen manager and CEO. Four full time hires to replace one burnt-out business owner, who had become the hardest-working, lowest paid person in his own company.

In my book *Big Ideas...For Small Businesses*, I encouraged every small business owner to think like a FTSE 250 company and produce an organisational chart:

> *"Every business should have an org chart – a flowchart that shows the company structure and hierarchy. You need to know*

who does what and who answers to whom... so you can see how the flow of responsibility runs through the company, and if something goes wrong, you know exactly whose responsibility it is to fix.

Don't be put off by thinking you don't need an org chart because you work on your own or you've only got a small team – all of these roles still need filling even if it's your name that you're putting next to each role within the organisation.

When I first started out, I was head of marketing, bookkeeper, web designer, copywriter, payroll, managing director, tea boy, customer service department, salesman, admin assistant and chief pot washer.

But then, as I grew, I was able to delegate some of those roles and responsibilities, and suddenly other people's names started to appear on my org chart... As I write this now, my org chart has 27 different roles on it and my name is only next to three of them – shareholder, MD and marketing director.

If I wanted to completely remove myself from the business, I would need to hire an MD and a marketing director. I would then have my name next to just one role within the organisation – that of shareholder."

It's been six years since I wrote those words and my org chart has evolved. I managed to remove myself further thanks to my False EXIT, promoting one of my team to Chief Operating Officer (effectively the MD role I was previously fulfilling), and hiring a self-driven marketer to carry much of the weight of my marketing director duties. This means that my primary role within the organisation is now "majority shareholder".

Take some time to plot out your own org chart. Consider every role within your company that needs to be fulfilled. Think in terms of job description first and foremost, so list "Admin, Marketing, and Customer Service" rather than "Anthony, Meredith, and Christopher" because in most small businesses, people (especially the business owner) often end up covering multiple roles. Start with roles, then add names to each role.

This is often a good opportunity to strategize. Once the roles are set in stone, you can play around with different people in different roles. Put your org chart on a whiteboard and see what happens if you rub some names out, swap some people around or bring in some new blood. Remember Jim Collins' words as you do this – "The right people on the bus, the wrong people off the bus and the right people in the right seats."

This is your chance to play Fantasy Bus Driver. Once the seats are set in stone, you can (virtually) kick passengers off the bus, invite superior ones to replace them and ask anyone you like to swap seats or even sit in multiple seats. Just be careful not to leave your fantasy org chart on display in the team canteen – no one wants to see that the boss's vision for the future doesn't include them.

TO OUTSOURCE OR NOT?

What if you don't fancy filling a bus though? Why not just book a taxi when you need one? A private hire vehicle with a highly trained driver who specialises in taking people exactly where they need to go?

In other words, do you recruit in-house or outsource to a third party? This is a dilemma that many ambitious, lifestyle business owners battle with. You understand the old saying, "If you want to go fast, go alone. If you want to go far, go with others", but the thought of recruiting and managing a team of people makes your skin crawl. You didn't go into business to become a manager – you started your venture with your dream lifestyle very much in mind. You've no desire to be tied to an office or even to office hours. The idea that you would be answerable to a team of employees, unable to take a morning off without permission is sacrilegious to you. Score one point for outsourcing.

But what will other people think? After all, aren't *proper* businesses supposed to employ people? If you work from home, farming out tasks on an ad-hoc basis to freelancers and trusted third parties, won't you look like small fry?

Well, the more clearly you can define what your own ambitious, lifestyle business looks like, the less you'll care what other people think and the more you'll realise there is no "right" way of running your business – there's only *your* way. Running an ambitious, lifestyle business isn't about optimising for maximum efficiency and profits from the business. Instead, it's about optimising for the best *lifestyle* for you, the business owner. That could mean outsourcing everything or it could mean building a large in-house team. *You* decide.

My friends Mark and Nick are polar opposites when it comes to recruitment. Mark has offices in Plymouth and London, and employs more than 20 members of staff, with a turnover in excess of £2million.

By contrast, Nick employs no one. He used to have a business partner, a small team, and an office to house them all in – all of which made him miserable and unprofitable. Now, Nick works as a lone wolf; aided and abetted by a collection of hand-picked freelancers. He works from home, keeping hours that suit him, doing work he loves. He's able to go to the gym every morning, takes regular half-days to go sailing, and enjoys long weekends at his holiday home in Devon. Because Nick works alone, only paying out for freelancers as and when he's already won the business to pay for them, the majority of his £400,000-plus turnover is profit.

Both Nick and Mark extract a similar amount of profit from their businesses yet achieve that profit by very different means. Once again, there's no right way, only the right way for *you*. If Mark and Nick were to swap roles one thing's for sure – they'd both hate it!

I remember once grumbling to Nick that my team wasn't following the systems I'd put in place. "You see, this is why I don't employ anyone," he replied. "When you pay someone a salary, they get paid regardless of how good their work is, how long they take or whether they even do what you ask. But when you outsource, that person only gets paid when the work is done – and done right. There's no incentive for your team to do what *you* want. Sure, you might moan at them every now and then, and yes, you could maybe take their job away if they're really bad, but the freelancer has that incentive in place permanently – do it right, on time, or don't get paid. You can't underestimate that."

This really hit home with me. When I had a team of 15, I was paying people to sit around the office watching Disney films for "research", chatting to their friends or pushing bits of paper around a desk, doing work that *they* wanted to do rather than what I'd asked them to do – the work that paid the bills, including their salary. Eventually, I did take away their jobs, but not until they'd burned through a huge pile of my cash and left me with no choice but to stop paying them.

By contrast, when I've outsourced, I don't pay for procrastination. If they want to sit around staring into space, great, they can do it on their time. I'm hiring them to do a specific job and they're only going to get paid when they deliver that job. They're also only going to get paid if they deliver the work to the standard I've asked and on time. Once again, the incentive is key. Employees get their next pay almost regardless of what they do, while a freelancer's only arrives when they deliver on their promises.

To repeat what I said at the start of this chapter, my dream number of employees is zero. I say this despite having a small team because while I do now employ some amazing people, I've had to kiss an awful lot of frogs to get here. In order to assemble a team of five who do great work, I've hired and fired more than 30. That's 25 employees I've wasted time, money and energy recruiting, training, managing, nagging, coaching, losing sleep over, pulling my hair out in frustration over, and eventually firing.

Thirty people to build a team of five superstars. That's a hit rate of just one in six. I thought every single one of the 30 I hired were going to work out just fine. I certainly didn't foresee letting 25 of them go – most for a notable loss on the P/L statement; some significantly so with many failed hires not only losing money while in situ, but also being paid to leave with either a few months' notice or many thousands in redundancy payments.

It's pretty clear which camp I fall into. In an ideal world, like Nick, I wouldn't employ *anyone*. I would simply farm out work to experts on a piecemeal basis, paying them on delivery of work well done. If they don't deliver, I don't pay. If their quality slips, I use someone else. And if they do a great job, I look after them really well.

But that's what works for me. That's what suits *my* ambitious, lifestyle business. You may be a better manager than me (most people are), and if so, like Mark, you may be far more suited to building your own in-house team. Or you may choose a hybrid model, outsourcing until it's cheaper to bring in the job in-house, only hiring when it's too painful or too time-consuming not to.

So should you outsource or hire in-house? You tell me.

"I'M JUST LIKE STEVE JOBS, REALLY"

According to biographer Walter Isaacson, Apple founder Steve Jobs "could have been one of the world's worst managers".

Isaacson explained that Jobs was "very petulant… very brittle. He could be very, very mean to people at times. Whether it was to a waitress in a restaurant or to a guy who had stayed up all night coding. He was a pretty abrasive… cantankerous character."

There aren't many ways I'm comparable to Steve Jobs, but "one of the world's worst managers" is unfortunately one of them.

I'm a terrible manager. If I didn't own the business, I wouldn't be allowed anywhere near a management position with a very large bargepole. It's hardly surprising that, having employed dozens and dozens of people across all my businesses, more than 80% of them have quit or been fired, with most failing to last a year.

Unlike Jobs, I'm not rude to waitresses, but I can certainly be petulant and cantankerous when managing team members. I feel as if each minute spent managing is 60 seconds stolen from my own goals, my own drive, my own focus. I found myself answering the team's questions all day long – questions that appear to me to have such blindingly obvious answers or are so unimportant or inconsequential that I can't fathom why they're wasting everyone's time even considering them.

One of my mentors once told me: "Managing people is really simple. Just tell them, *very clearly,* what you want. Then, once you've verified that they've done it well, praise them." He also warned me: "It may be simple. But it's not easy." How right he was! Those few sentences explain all the reasons I'm a bad manager: I don't define what I want clearly enough, I don't verify enough and I don't praise enough.

"Once they've done it well, praise them"? Sure, I'll praise them, I thought, *if* they ever do what I ask, let alone do it well! I was convinced that *they* were the problem. *They* weren't listening. *They* didn't care. *They* thought they knew better. And then, I got an eight-week old cockapoo, called Chewie.

Chewie and I went to puppy classes, where we learned the basics of dog training. "Training a dog is really simple," said Cassie, the trainer. "Just tell them, *very clearly,* what you want. Then, once you've verified that they've done it well, praise them."

A tiny puppy obviously isn't going to understand English, let alone read your mind. So you physically demonstrate what you want, while giving a very clear command, and wait for the pup to copy you. When he does, he's rewarded with a hunk of sausage meat. It's called positive reinforcement and it works brilliantly. With a twirl of my finger, I can make Chewie spin on the spot. If an Amazon driver knocks on the door, Chewie runs to his bed, patiently awaiting his reward. If we're walking off-lead and he strays too far from me, I can simply raise my hand in the air and whistle and he'll come sprinting back to me.

Why? Because I've trained him to do so. I've given him positive reinforcement for each of those situations. When I give this *very clear* instruction (twirl the finger; knock on the front door; raise my arm and whistle), Chewie knows what's expected of him. The instruction has to be very clear. If I want him to stop chasing a rabbit while on a walk, my command is to put my arm in the air and whistle. It isn't to yell: "Chewie! Stop that! Oh bloody hell! Stop it! Come here! Why are you doing that? Get back here now. You know you're not meant to do that!"

Positive reinforcement is praise or reward for a job well done. It works with dogs and with humans. Try it on your teenager if you don't believe me. Instead of nagging them to tidy their room, give them a chocolate bar each time they bring some dirty washing out of their cesspit. You may have to wait a while for the opportunity to reinforce this particular behaviour, though.

Even on the rare occasions when I *think* I'm being a good manager, my "resting Roy Keane face" betrays my true feelings.

Former Manchester United and Republic of Ireland footballer Roy Keane was one of the best players of his generation and spent eight years as United captain. He was described by legendary manager Sir Alex Ferguson as "a man whose intensity could intimidate his team-mates, but a great leader on the pitch".

Keane may have been a great leader on the pitch, but his managerial career off it never reached the same heights. Despite winning promotion to the Premier League in his first season as Sunderland boss, Keane resigned the following year with the Black Cats having lost five of their last six matches. The Sunderland players were rumoured to have celebrated when they heard news of his resignation because his harsh, unforgiving management style wasn't popular with them. A few uneventful seasons at Ipswich Town followed, with Keane sacked in January 2011. That was the end of his managerial career.

Instead, Keane turned his hand to a career in the media. With his no-nonsense, tell-it-as-it-is, uncompromising viewpoints, he's the perfect foil to a middle-of-the-road pundit rolling out tired old "game-of-two-halves" cliches. Next time Roy's on the telly, watch his face closely. Study his emotions and reactions. Of course, he's never been too shy to tell people exactly what he thinks of them to their face. But even without talking, his face paints a thousand (very angry) words – whether that be a grimace, a grit of the teeth, a roll of the eyes or a stern shake of the head.

This probably explains why Roy Keane doesn't manage people any more. It certainly explains why I shouldn't. Every time I'm asked: "Boss, what do you think of this wonderful idea I've had?", I'd reply: "Erm, yeah, interesting. We *could* do something like that in the future I suppose. But how are you getting on with our current plan?"

But it's too late. My resting Roy Keane face has already kicked in, and broadcasted my true thoughts, which are: "What the fuck? This has got to be, hands-down, the worst idea I've ever heard. No wonder you can't hit your targets if that's the kind of shite you've got swimming around that tiny brain of yours. You're supposed to be a professional. Pah!"

Thankfully, I've learned *not* to manage people. The right people don't need managing, of course. But by sharing my clearly defined, lived-and-breathed vision and values, giving my team my decision-making framework, as well as a support system of established proven processes, this tells them, very clearly, what I want. All that remains for me to do is verify that they've done it well (you'll learn systems to automate that shortly), and praise them – leaving me free to lead rather than manage.

Steve Jobs and Roy Keane were both successful, inspirational leaders, but terrible managers. I can take heart from that. My managerial incompetence needn't prevent me from making a False EXIT (in fact, my absence probably helps). I just need to make sure that my team is well led. And guess what? I don't need to be there for that, either.

LEADING A LEGACY

When Bill Gates stepped down from his full-time role at Microsoft in 2008, the company was valued at $173billion. By the end of 2021, 13 years without Gates' leadership led to a market cap of $2.52trillion – a more than 14-fold increase.

"World's worst manager" Steve Jobs passed away in 2011 with Apple's worth at $350billion. A decade later, the post-Jobs era resulted in a seven-fold gain to $2.64trillion.

Jobs and Gates are synonymous with Apple and Microsoft. You'd be forgiven for thinking that the company's fortunes would be forever tied to these inspirational founders and their unique leadership styles. Not so. Both exited the day-to-day, but the legacy of their leadership lives on. Employees at Apple are as influenced today, years after his death, by Jobs' culture of innovation, innate usability, and elegant design as they were during his tenure. Likewise, the culture Bill Gates instilled at

Microsoft, of optimism (remember, Internet Explorer had the balls to ask to be your default browser), collaboration and innovation remain long after he departed. Jobs and Gates may have exited, but their vision and values remain.

Of course, there are far more examples of companies who abandon their founder's values the minute they leave the building. So how do we ensure *our* vision and values remain intact? How can we plan our legacy before we leave?

Warren Buffett, the 92-year-old chairman of multinational conglomerate Berkshire Hathaway, gets asked this question a lot. His answer?

> *"I will keep working until about five years after I die, and I've given the directors a ouija board so they can keep in touch. But if the ouija board doesn't work, we have outstanding people who can do what I do."*

Buffett delivers a one-two punch of a great soundbite with incredible wisdom. Sure, jokes about ouija boards and working from beyond the grave raise a smile, but while you're chuckling, Warren tells you the truth:

> *"...we have outstanding people who can do what I do."*

Berkshire Hathaway has the right people. It has clearly defined core values that are lived and breathed: growth, authenticity, empowerment, relationships, compassion, and service. It has its founder's wishes at its heart. In a 15-page letter entitled *Berkshire – Past, Present and Future*, Buffett explains his thought process at key points in the company's history from the "monumentally stupid decision" he made not to sell his Berkshire shares in 1964 (because the buyer reneged on a verbally agreed price) to refusing to sugar coat the "bad news" that Berkshire's long-term gains "will not come close to those achieved in the past 50 years".

Buffett adds that "no company will be more shareholder-minded than Berkshire" and signs off with a reminder to himself as much as those who have trusted him with their hard-earned money:

> *"I am a lucky fellow to have you as partners*
>
> *– Warren E. Buffett"*

The right people may not need managing, but they still need leading. You can lead remotely, automatically, and even from beyond the grave – as long as your people can correctly answer one question.

At Berkshire Hathaway it is: "What would Warren do?"

At Apple, it's: "What would Steve do?"

At Microsoft, they ask: "What would Bill do?"

And at your company, what would *you* do?

6. DECISION-MAKING FRAMEWORK

"Build a man a fire and he'll be warm for a day. Set a man on fire and he'll be warm for the rest of his life,"

–Sir Terry Pratchett

I hope you're feeling positive about the prospect of a False EXIT now. You've worked on your vision and values, and you know how to get the right people on your bus (as well as ensuring you've got the right people in the right seats!). That's great. But I'm afraid there's still more work to be done.

Because at this point, all those right people, who share your values and buy into your vision, are poised, ready to spring into action. They've just got one question: "What do we do now, boss?"

To truly remove yourself from the day-to-day operations, you'll need your team to be capable of competently making decisions, ideally reaching the same conclusion you would. It's important, therefore, to establish a solid decision-making framework that they all know how to follow.

I'M SORRY, GOD ISN'T HERE RIGHT NOW. PLEASE LEAVE YOUR PRAYERS AFTER THE TONE.

All I know about history, I learned from Blackadder. All I know about philosophy, I learned from The Good Place. And everything I know about religion, I learned from Bruce Almighty.

The 2003 film sees Jim Carrey play Bruce Nolan, a TV reporter who blames God for everything bad that happens to him. Even stepping in a puddle is God's fault. He moans…a lot.

Eventually, God (played by Morgan Freeman) gets fed up with Bruce's whining and takes matters into his own divine hands, popping down to Earth to meet Bruce:

> *"You've been doing a lot of complaining about me, Bruce. And quite frankly, I'm tired of it… I brought you here to offer you a job… my job. You think you can do it better, so here's your chance. When you leave this building, you will be endowed with all my powers."*

Hilarity and special effects abound, as Bruce uses and abuses his new-found powers in order to advance his career, part the red sea (of soup), and even make his girlfriend's breasts larger.

But of course, with divine power, comes divine responsibility. Bruce starts to hear voices in his head.

God (well, Morgan Freeman) tells him: "They're prayers, Bruce. You keep ignoring them and they're going to build up on you like that. You didn't think being God was going to be all fun and games, did you?"

Bruce decides that he needs organisation and management. He says: "I need a system. Something concrete. Let all prayers be organised into files." Hey presto: Bruce's living room is suddenly packed out with filing cabinets, but there's no room to move.

"I know – prayer Post-its!" Instantly, everything in the room (including Bruce and Sam the dog) is covered in Post-it notes.

Like most small business owners before him, Bruce then thinks that email could be his saviour. He sits at his computer: "You've got 1,527,503 unread prayers." He then works – at superhuman speed, of course – day and night to clear the emails. But when he checks, his inbox is up to three million-plus.

Frustrated, he tries a shortcut. He ticks Reply To All and writes just one word – "Yes". And then hundreds of thousands of people win the lottery, short people become taller, the stock market triples and people lose weight eating doughnuts.

But there are consequences to Bruce's actions, too – riots, a tsunami and, more personal, he gets dumped. Desperate, he pleads for God to take his powers back. And like every small business owner returning from a long weekend away, God comes back to save the day.

> *God: Not as easy as it looks, is it son, this God business? People want me to do everything for them. But what they don't realise is they have the power... I figure you can handle things now.*
>
> *Bruce: But what if I need you? What if I have questions?*
>
> *God: That's your problem, Bruce. That's everybody's problem. You keep looking up.*

Is that everybody's problem in *your* company? Does everyone keep looking up – to you – for the answer to every question they might have? Have you made yourself God; the almighty ruler, who sees everything and knows the answer to every question? A divine being to whom everyone looks for guidance, unable to take a few days off without the "What should I do about x?" questions backing up and no prospect of ever reaching inbox zero?

If so, maybe you should consider how God tackles this problem in the real world. Bruce was spot on when he said that "organisation and management is what I need". But filing cabinets, Post-it notes and email are not the answer.

When you are the person that everyone goes to for answers, you need really good systems. God has world-class systems. For starters, He's got a really comprehensive book which answers pretty much any question anyone could ever have. It's the bestselling book of all time. You're one of eight billion people living on the planet, so rather than waiting in line to speak to the one person with the answers, you can simply read His book.

Want some help applying what's written in the book to your specific circumstances? Why not visit one of God's local branches, where one of His senior executives, who have dedicated their lives to the interpretation of the book, will help you connect the dots and translate the ancient text for modern day life.

No time to read the book or pop into your local branch? Not to worry, God's put together a nice handy checklist for you with a top ten do's and don'ts to follow. A TL/DR (too long, didn't read) for life. Yet another system which means He doesn't need to spend all His time answering those, "What should I do, God?" prayers.

As Morgan Freeman's portrayal of God tells us: "People want me to do everything for them. But what they don't realise is *they* have the power." The book, the organisation, the structure, and the commandments all serve the same purpose: giving *you* the power to make your own decisions. They're the world's largest decision-making framework.

If He can create a decision-making framework for eight billion people (yes, I know we don't all share the same beliefs, but the framework is there, whether or not we choose or want to use it), then we should be able to create one for our small business.

Most people know that Sir Isaac Newton discovered the universal law of gravity. We all learned about the apple falling from the tree as kids. Well, Newton actually oversaw the emergence of modern science throughout the 16th and 17th centuries. He was the first to draw parallels between abstract mathematical concepts and the physical world around us.

Before Newton, people thought that God was responsible for everything. Why did the apple fall from the tree? Because God made it fall. Newton proved that there was a mathematical principle (gravity) which would universally apply, causing all apples to fall. However, disproving the theory that God made the apple fall didn't lead to a rise in atheism. After all, why would the all-powerful God concern himself with the fate of a single apple when He could create a fundamental worldwide law – gravity – which would cause *all* apples to fall?

We need to spark a Newtonian-style revolution in our teams to shift their thinking from, "Let's find out what the boss wants to do about x" to "What framework has the boss created which will tell *us* what to do about x?" – from "The boss made the apple fall" to "The boss's framework makes apples fall" – making them realise that they have the power.

As I said earlier, to remove yourself from the day-to-day operations, you'll need your team to be capable of competently making decisions and reaching the same conclusions you would. This is why your vision and values are so important. If your team knows the big, overarching why – the company's reason for existing – then it's far more likely they will arrive at the "right" answer than left to their own devices.

If you keep giving your team the answer to a problem, they'll be able to solve that problem. But when you show them *how* to solve that problem, they'll be able to solve almost *any* problem. And if you hand your team a clearly defined framework for making decisions, then they'll solve more problems, more accurately, faster, and without requiring you as the font of all knowledge.

But first, let's check this decision doesn't need to be made by you.

YES, MR. PRESIDENT!

Imagine you're the President of the United States – the most powerful person on the planet. What you say, goes. Feels good, doesn't it? But don't forget that 330million Americans are relying on you to make the big calls, with life-changing consequences for every single one of them. How will you manage the economy, tackle unemployment, improve healthcare, look after the elderly, and defend your borders? That's just one morning's decision-making work in the Oval Office.

In an article for medium.com, former President Barack Obama wrote that: "No decision that landed on my desk had an easy, tidy answer. The black-and-white questions never made it to me – somebody else on my staff would have already answered them."

POTUS (President of the United States) level decision making – where the easy-to-answer, inconsequential decisions don't reach your desk – is essential for your False EXIT. Once you've left the day-to-day, you'll rarely be at your desk, let alone sat there answering small fry questions all day long.

So, how do you decide what a POTUS-level decision is? This depends on your financial situation, how well you trust your team, their ability to calculate probability, and your overall attitude to risk. For most people, putting a pounds-and-pence figure on POTUS decisions helps. For my own decision-making framework, I use three figures:

1. Under £50. If making an incorrect decision would result in a loss of less than £50, I don't want to know about it. I trust you to make an informed, probability-based decision that should negate the loss, but a few £50 losses here and there aren't going to break the bank for me.

2. £50 to £500. I still trust my team to make the right call on these decisions but I want to review these calls. To avoid being a bottleneck in my business, I review them *after* they've already been made by the team. This could be a weekly or monthly review, depending on the number of decisions the team are making.
3. £500 to £5,000. Now the consequences of bad decisions are getting serious. First, you need to ask: is this decision reversible? If so, you can follow the same process as a £50 to £500 call. As long as you're confident in your decision, then I'll review it after you've made your call, knowing I can always veto or amend it later without fatal damage. If it's not reversible however, then it's a POTUS-level decision.

Anything above £5,000 and any irreversible decision over £500 is POTUS level. (For the sake of clarity, I am POTUS in my business – I'm not passing these things over to Obama or Joe Biden, and certainly not Donald Trump). I want to make those calls – or to be more accurate, I want the help of my team to make those calls.

I want to hear *their* decision-making framework. Document the conundrum for me, lay out the options, everything you've considered, and which way you're leaning. Imagine you've got 30 seconds with the President to explain the problem and leave with an answer (hopefully the right one). How prepared are you? How succinct and accurately do you lay out your presentation?

Once you've explained the decision-making framework you've used, I now want to know how confident you are that you already have the right answer. I'm not talking about unfounded bravado, the type displayed by project managers in The Apprentice who ignore market research, their team, and industry experts, instead opting to go for their own wacky idea that they're "100% sure" is the best option. I'm talking about an accurate appraisal of the probability of making the right call.

"Because every tough decision came down to a probability then certainty was an impossibility, which could leave me encumbered by the sense I could never get it quite right," explains President Obama. "So rather than let myself get paralysed in the quest for a perfect solution, or succumb to the temptation to just go with my gut every time, I created a sound decision-making process — one where I listened to the experts, followed the facts, considered my goals and weighed all of that against my principles."

Even with hundreds of staff, access to world-renowned experts and any data he would like to get his hands on, President Obama often had to make decisions that seemed like a coin toss. Remember, the easy decisions never reached his desk. He was only ever making the tough, literally POTUS-level decisions. In those cases, his aim was to swap certainty for probability.

He knew that when 100% certainty was impossible, but you still have to make a decision, even a 51% edge tips the scales in your favour. Clearly, President Obama wasn't betting the farm on a 51% chance of success. But 51% enabled him to act decisively and be at peace he'd made the best call with the information available.

I ask my team to aim for 80% certainty. This demonstrates to them that I understand 100% certainty is BS, but also that I trust their judgement *if* they are fairly accurate at calculating probabilities. Most people aren't. Most people think about probability in terms of one of three black-or-white outcomes:

1. Will happen.
2. Won't happen.
3. Might happen.

But what happens if you try to allocate a percentage to those three outcomes? Most people's estimates of probability versus certainty vary greatly. If the weather forecast says there's a 25% chance of rain today, do you think it won't rain or that it might rain? What about if there's a 5% chance? Or 95%?

Well, if you leave your umbrella at home every time there's a 5% chance of rain, you're going to get wet once every 20 times because you've selected the "won't happen" option.

Asking my team for an estimated 80% chance of success places them on the border of their "might happen" and "will happen" ranges, so I'm making them think consciously why it's *not* a 100% slam dunk. Of course, you may need to play with the percentages for your team, depending on whether they're hope-for-the-best optimists or I-knew-it-wouldn't-work pessimists. Ideally, you'll have a team of entirely rational, highly accurate probability gaugers that you can trust to make decisions with a high level of success. How confident are you that this is the case?

Remember, the right people – who share your vision and values, armed with the right decision-making framework – can usually be trusted to make good decisions. US department store chain Nordstrom gave new employees a copy of its staff "handbook" – a five-by-eight inch laminated card, which read:

> *"Welcome to Nordstrom.*
>
> *Our number one goal is to provide outstanding customer service.*
>
> *Set both your personal and professional goals high. We have great confidence in your ability to achieve them.*
>
> *Nordstrom Rules:*

Rule #1: Use your good judgement in all situations.

There will be no additional rules."

Founder Jim Nordstrom said of this high level of trust shown in his team: "We view our people as professionals. They don't need rules. They need basic guideposts, but not rules. You can do anything you need to at Nordstrom to get the job done, just so long as you live up to our basic values and standards."

You're POTUS. Your job is to make a few tough decisions, while being able to trust your team to make the majority of calls. Everything below POTUS level is decided by your team members with help from the decision-making framework, their peers – or maybe from Mr Chairman.

WHAT DO YOU THINK, MR CHAIRMAN?

For one of our One Percent Club coaching calls, I was honoured to welcome Simon Hallett, the former chief investment officer of US investment house Harding Loevner. (He also happens to be the chairman of my beloved Plymouth Argyle football club).

We discussed using data to make better decisions and I asked Simon to give his view on how small business owners can reach the many conclusions they must each day when they cannot identify the 51-49 edge. He answer was revealing:

"We ask two questions:

Is the decision consequential?

Is the decision reversible?

If a decision is difficult to make, but the consequences are trivial, I toss a coin. I'm not even kidding – I literally toss a coin!

You want to devote your mental energy to decisions that are consequential and irreversible. If they're reversible or inconsequential, and you get it wrong – so what!"

The idea that decisions within a professional football club run by an investment banker could be made on the toss of a coin seemed ludicrous at first.

However, flipping a coin for an inconsequential or reversible decision reduces analysis paralysis, thus enabling your team to make quicker decisions (without you) – and more of them. More rapidly made decisions equals a faster feedback loop, helping to compound gains from the good calls and cutting losses from the bad ones far sooner.

Resource allocation is all about risk versus reward. The ideal scenario is a tiny amount of risk for potentially unlimited rewards. Very little downside for an uncapped upside.

There are an abundance of such risk/reward opportunities in the inconsequential/reversible quadrant:

CONSEQUENTIAL & REVERSIBLE AIM FOR 80% CLARITY	**CONSEQUENTIAL & IRREVERSIBLE** POTUS DECISION
INCONSEQUENTIAL & REVERSIBLE TOSS A COIN	**INCONSEQUENTIAL & IRREVERSIBLE** WHY BOTHER?

Years ago, I knew two young lads who went into business together. They split the business straight down the middle, becoming equal

50% shareholders. This seemed fair to both partners, who agreed that they would split everything – all the work, all the rewards, all the late nights, all the limelight and, of course, all the decision making.

What happens, though, when they disagree on a course of action? When one wants to go left and the other right? Well, these two chaps decided to embrace a similar technique to Simon Hallett.

Trusting their partner enough to be certain that the potential consequences of the other person's decision wouldn't be catastrophic (and possibly reversible), these two plucky lads decided to give the deciding vote in any 50/50 deadlocked decision to "Mr Chairman", an independent third party, whose sole task was to have the final say on any split decisions.

From that day on, Mr Chairman sat in their boardroom for every single meeting, not once uttering a word in support (or criticism) of either man. At all times, Mr Chairman remained stoically silent. Very rarely called into action, Mr Chairman was always prepared to cast the decisive vote should he be called upon.

Usually, the partners would present their case, concede arguments, and come to a consensus between them. But on the rare occasions they couldn't reach an agreement, they knew it was time to turn to Mr Chairman.

"Do you want heads or tails?"

Mr Chairman was a fifty pence piece. The very first coin that the boys received in exchange for selling their wares was put aside, framed, and displayed on the boardroom wall – with the plaque: "Mr Chairman. Money talks – and what he says, goes!"

It may seem strange for you to chance the fate of your company on the toss of a coin. But remember, you're only going to ask Mr Chairman to help make inconsequential, reversible decisions – those with low risk and potentially high rewards. Heads you win, tails you don't lose.

VISION AND VALUES FOR DECISION MAKING

Clearly defined, lived-and-breathed vision and values shared by everyone in the business make it incredibly easy for your team to make vision or values-driven decisions.

> *Should Riverford Organic Farms sell blueberries in winter?*
>
> *Should the All Blacks select a highly talented winger who's also a bit of a dickhead?*
>
> *Should I refund a customer who hasn't noticed they're overpaying?*

Thanks to vision and values, we already know the answer to all of these.

Of course, not every decision can be answered purely based on your vision or values. "Should we borrow £150,000 to acquire this complimentary business?" Well, that depends on a lot more than simply "does this fit our core values?" and would, of course, be a POTUS-level decision. But many of the questions your team are looking to you to answer could be easily answered automatically by signposting to the appropriate value(s).

Next time someone in your business asks you an easy question, don't give them the answer. Instead, steer them to the vision or value that will help them discover the answer for themselves. Or better, discover what they think the right answer is before saying anything: "What do you think?" Then, follow up with: "Why do you say that?" Keep asking why until they arrive at one of your values.

Before long, they'll soon realise that, as Morgan Freeman's God told us, "They have the power" and no longer need to "look up" for the answers.

Here's an example from my information marketing business that has "improving people's lives with knowledge and information" as its vision, and trustworthiness as one of its core values:

> *Team Member: "I've found a target market that could be quite lucrative. Do you think we should launch this new product?"*
>
> *Me: "What are your thoughts?"*
>
> *Team Member: "Well, as I say, it's a potentially lucrative market. It's untested though, so I'm not sure if it would really help people."*
>
> *Me: "Why?"*
>
> *Team Member: "There's nothing like it out there. If it does work though, I'm confident it will be popular."*
>
> *Me: "How could we find out if it would genuinely improve people's lives?" [Note my labelling of the vision or value I want them to use in their decision-making process].*
>
> *Team Member: "I could put together a small-scale MVP (Minimum Viable Product) with a focus group and see if it helps them?"*
>
> *Me: "That sounds good."*

I don't give them the solution but instead ask vision and values-related questions until the team member reaches their own values-driven answer. The more you give answers, the more people will come to you for answers. Throw questions back at them (especially the same question: "What do our core values say about this?"), and they'll soon realise they can reach the same answer quicker and easier without asking you.

GUIDELINES FOR DECISION MAKING

> *"I think it should be orange."*
>
> *"I like green."*
>
> *"I saw a pink one the other day. Pink is nice, isn't it?"*
>
> *"I don't like pink. It was my ex's favourite colour."*

My team was discussing which colour the button should be on a new sales page we were launching. Meanwhile, I repeated the words "Kill. Me. Now." in my head and pondered a million other far more productive things I could be doing with my time.

> *"Erm, can I make a radical suggestion?" I asked.*
>
> *"Sure..."*
>
> *"How about we use hex code #ab10de, with white, size 12 sans-serif font in all-caps?"*

Cue a sea of blank faces.

> *"You know, the agreed call-to-action button colour as laid out in our brand guidelines..."*

Heuristics such as brand guidelines, a sales script, or agreed terminology (for example, the phrases "on this occasion" and "as a gesture of goodwill" are banned in our customer service department), ensures no time is wasted having decision-by-committee debates. They also ensure your brand is represented by a refined, optimised pipeline, rather than whatever bucket an individual member of staff has in their hand that particular day.

Don't get me wrong ; choosing the "right" colour of a button can make a huge difference to the conversion rate on a high-traffic website. But it shouldn't be decided on a whim and certainly not based on what a handful of people think or like.

Changing the button changes the pipeline. It's your job to constantly improve the pipeline and your team's job to ensure they consistently use the pipeline.

This is one of many guiding principles that I share with my team. Others include:

1. We truly live up to our core values of fun, trustworthiness, and community.
2. We are an ambitious, lifestyle business. We're deliberately small, choosing to work remotely and flexibly.
3. We work on a "HIIT" (High Intensity Interval Training) basis – we sprint, then we rest.
4. We carry no passengers. There's no such thing as "not my job" in this job.
5. We work hard creating evergreen assets and shoot fish in a barrel during marketing campaigns, so that we don't have to work hard the rest of the time.
6. We plan our work in 90-day chunks. And we stick to the plan, focusing on just *one* thing for those 90 days.
7. Everybody in the business owns their own one thing (one goal that takes priority over everything else), as well as their own individual three metrics.

8. We're a systems-run business. The systems run the business. We operate the systems.
9. We are our members' Trusted Advisor.
10. We aim to never lose a customer. If we do, we've failed them and haven't been their Trusted Advisor.
11. Our aim isn't moon shots; it's constant, never-ending improvement of the pipeline, upgrading the systems that run the business, and aiming to be 1% better each week.
12. We're all here to succeed and grow. We improve ourselves by 1% each week too.

Now that's quite a lot for new team members to take in at once. This is why I've created an internal nurture sequence, delivering a fortnightly email, each one telling a different story relating to a specific guiding principle:

- How I discovered the ambitious, lifestyle business ethos after previously working 100-plus-hour work weeks.
- How we've demonstrated we are our members' Trusted Advisor by doing the right thing, even though we made less money.
- What happened when the systems went wrong or weren't followed.

I can refer my team to these principles at any point to help them make better decisions. After a major marketing campaign, when a team member is looking to keep busy during a quiet period, I can simply point to our HIIT principle and they'll know to ease off the gas, because we'll be sprinting again soon. Faced with the dilemma of a member who has accidentally been paying twice but hasn't noticed, I don't need to tell them what the "right thing" is. I simply need to ask: "What would their Trusted Advisor do?"

My favourite principle to signpost is the pipeline itself. Any member of my team will tell you, I utter the words "Where's the system for that?" or "What does your system look like?" on an almost daily basis. If something's gone wrong: "Why did the system fail us there?"

Again, I'm not giving any answers. I'm asking questions that signpost the framework I feel will help the person find the answer. Giving answers is carrying buckets. My job is to build a pipeline of decision-making frameworks, not to fetch buckets of answers.

WHAT DO *YOU* THINK?

If you recruit the right people, who share the same values as you, and make them intimately familiar with your guiding principles, then there's a very good chance they'll make good decisions most of the time – especially if you help them develop the muscle-memory of making their own decisions by using the decision-making framework pipeline.

By regularly reviewing the non-POTUS decisions that your team has made, you'll soon spot those who think like you and those who don't. Crucially, those who have made "bad" calls *shouldn't* be told that they made the "wrong" decision, but rather be asked plenty of questions as to why and how they reached their decision. If their answer doesn't reference your vision, a core value or decision-making framework, then that's the first place to look – "Which framework did you use to make that decision?"

Similarly, it's vital to use positive reinforcement and publicly praise the good decisions that were made in your absence, again signposting their use of the decision-making-framework which made it such a good call.

It's vital to praise in public and shame in private. When someone makes a great call, you want to put them on a pedestal and shine a light on them. When they make a bad call, you want to pull them aside and gently let them know they got it wrong and why. No one wants to be publicly shamed for making bad decisions – plus that leads to a fear of making *any* decision and builds the muscle memory of, "I'm just going to ask the boss every time". You want your team to get comfortable making decisions without you.

Even for the POTUS-level decisions that land on your desk, it's worthwhile getting feedback from your team on what they would do and why. You don't need to agree with them, of course (that's the beauty of being POTUS), but you should want to hear their thoughts and more importantly, their thought process, which is what you can influence.

Discussing high-level decisions with your team, demonstrating how you use the decision-making frameworks, will also help cement it in their mind next time they have *any* decision to make.

TICK TOCK, TICK TOCK!

I'm pretty terrible at making snap decisions. Give me 24 hours to ponder and I can make a good decision on pretty much any tough call. But present me with a problem that requires an immediate answer and you'd be better off asking Mr Chairman. Even his 50% strike rate is likely to beat mine when making snap judgements.

There will be curveballs in your business. There will be time-limited opportunities and there will be unexpected events which need fixing *right now*. Most can still be answered using your values and vision statement, and decision-making framework. If they're below a certain value, you would trust your team (assuming they consist of the right people) to make the right call in the moment, knowing you can review the decision later.

But what about the rare occasion when a POTUS-level decision is required immediately? Say, for example, we have the opportunity to buy £30,000 worth of stock for £18,000, but it's only available first-come, first served. What should the team do?

Well, in this scenario, I would hope that my team would flag it to me as a POTUS-level decision, but inform me that it requires an urgent decision. Knowing that a) I don't make good snap decisions and b) I may not be available or have the capacity to make such a crucial decision in time, in which case my default answer will always be no. I adopt the Hippocratic Oath of, "First, do no harm". What's the worst that could happen if I said yes? Well, I could commit to £18,000 of unexpected expenditure that I later realise I need for cashflow, be lumbered with a ton of stock that I can't shift, or find that I've bought stolen goods.

And what's the worst that can happen if I say no? I miss a good opportunity. That's it. No real harm done. Sure, I may have missed a chance to grow the business, but I haven't taken a risky chance which could harm it. A football team can always recover from failing to sign a great player. But signing a player they shouldn't have can hamper them for years. Ask any club relegated from the Premier League who are still lumbered with players on £100,000-plus a week contracts for the next three or four years.

My default answer is "no". I'm known as the Abominable No-man by my team. But would there be a scenario in which I would say yes to a time critical POTUS-level decision? Of course! If my own decision-making framework quickly and clearly leads me to that decision with a degree of certainty. This is key – you already have your own decision-making framework. You've been using it for years (or maybe decades), and follow it intuitively every time you make a decision. It's in your head and runs on autopilot.

Meanwhile, your team needs a little help, a little training, and a little guidance – in the form of a handy framework – to help make the process intuitive for them as well. Eventually, the less bucket-carrying decisions you make, referring them back to the decision-making framework pipeline to come up with the answers themselves, the more they'll build their muscle memory. Before long, they'll be doing so intuitively as well.

7. SYSTEMS

"Systems run the business and people run the systems,"

– Michael E. Gerber

HOW DO YOU SELL A BABY SHOP FOR £70MILLION?

On September 26th, 1974, Neville Wright bought a cloth for 37p, borrowed his dad's ladder, and started a window cleaning round. He then grew that tiny business into a £100million-plus empire, including selling online baby retailer Kiddicare.com to supermarket giant Morrisons for £70million in cash.

"So, how do you sell a baby shop for £70million? It was easy really," Neville told us on a One Percent Club coaching call. "We had systems for everything. If you don't develop systems, the opportunity to sell what you have created rarely happens. All the time I spent working on systems is probably the best investment I ever made."

This sounds great for a larger business like Kiddicare, but what if you're running a far smaller operation or are looking for a dream lifestyle False EXIT rather than a £70million payday?

Well, let's ask Neville to go back a few decades and tell us what his systems looked like when his business was still tiny:

> *"When I first started my window cleaning business, my system was straightforward: turn up at the agreed time, give a total price with no umming and ahhing, then do a good job for the price quoted. Simple.*

Disciplining myself to do that was easy, but when the business had grown to six people, I became a juggler, working alongside them, supervising them with my eyes and ears on overdrive.

With all of the systems existing purely in my head (as well as all the other jobs I had to do), this made me a bottleneck. I soon found out that if I were away for any reason, the business would slow down, and if I stayed away too long, it would eventually stop altogether."

It's a vicious circle. You need systems but you don't have time to create them because you're so busy fighting all the fires in your day-to-day operations. But the lack of systems is the very reason those fires exist and consume your time in the first place.

I'm afraid there's no silver bullet here. The only answer is to carve out time once your firefighting duties are complete to install some fire prevention systems.

You might want to highlight that last paragraph, because it's the first time in any of my books that I've advised you to simply work harder. There is no other answer though. Those fires still need putting out and without fire-prevention systems in place, more flames will demand your attention tomorrow and the day after – and every day for the rest of your career.

The best time to create systems was yesterday. The next best time is today. If you haven't got time today, that's because you didn't create the systems yesterday. If you want less firefighting tomorrow, do some fire prevention work today.

If you're going to exit the day-to-day, you won't be around to put the fires out so you need to become Chief Fire Prevention Officer in your business instead. Instead of carrying a bucket of water, ready to extinguish any fires, you'll install a robust, fully tested sprinkler system, which reaches every part of your business.

Instead of reacting to fires and solving problems for everyone else, you'll proactively use your experience and know-how to prevent fires from breaking out in the first place, ensuring your team is fully equipped and trained to deal with any fires as soon as they see a spark or smell smoke.

I became Chief Fire Prevention Officer for my business a full 18 months before I planned to exit the day-to-day. After a lifetime of putting out all the fires myself, I knew I had my work cut out to become a fully systems-run business.

In order to get his fire prevention systems out of his head and onto paper, Neville Wright needed to fully explain each process to someone in his team. Now, Neville is dyslexic and also has ADHD, which he embraces as a "great combination":

> *"It was great for building the businesses because there was no way I could waste my time sitting at a desk wondering how to spell anything (if I had tried, I would still be sitting there today, trying to figure out how to spell 'a-n-y-t-h-i-n-g').*
>
> *Transferring the business functions from my head onto paper was actually simple, but it really tested my patience because the person who actually documents it for me must understand every step of the process or it could all go tits up.*
>
> *All this detail is sometimes frustrating but absolutely necessary to save time in the long run and make more money repeatedly, easier and quicker once the processes are in place."*

Neville, whose company also saw his wife, daughters and a son-in-law involved in the day-to-day, employed a rather novel way of making sure everything transferred from his head onto paper – by playing "Dad's Dead", a game I described in *Routine Machine*:

> *"The rules were simple. For the rest of the working day, Neville was going to pretend to be dead.*
>
> *'Dad, how much do we charge for this product?'*
>
> *'No idea love, I'm dead.'*
>
> *'Dad, who's the best supplier for this new buggy range?'*
>
> *'Don't ask me, I'm dead.'*
>
> *'Dad, what's our login for online banking?'*
>
> *'Dead people don't know logins.'*
>
> *'Can you ask your dad to sign this form please?'*
>
> *'I'm sorry, he can't sign anything at the moment. He's dead.'*
>
> *After playing Dad's Dead, Neville made a full recovery (rumours of his death being greatly exaggerated) and was back at the helm the very next day. The first thing he did on the day of his resurrection was to ensure new systems and processes were put into place to remove him as the potential bottleneck.*
>
> *Decisions were automated up to a certain level. Documents like a staff handbook and how-to manuals were created so that all of Neville's years of knowledge and experience were available to the team without them having to have physical access to the man himself."*

By playing Dad's Dead, Neville made his business death-proof. If he had dropped dead (or taken a False EXIT) at any point from then on, the family business would have carried on without him seamlessly. Dad's Dead helped to plug the gaps between the documented systems and the ones in Neville's head.

It's a common problem when systemising a business. As the business owner, everything is in your head. As you attempt to document each process, you unintentionally leave out a crucial few steps that, to you, are painfully obvious and happen on autopilot. But the person following the step-by-step process needs *every* step mapped out in order for the process to make sense. This partial documenting of the systems in your head is like winking in the dark – you know exactly what you're doing but no one else does.

Neville's "great combination" of dyslexia and ADHD prevented him from documenting the processes himself, forcing him to explain them fully to a third party who would capture them comprehensively, so that *anyone* could follow. If Nev skips a vital step in his explanation, they can ask, "But what about x?" or "How do we get to y?" then fill in the gaps. If the gaps aren't obvious, a quick round of Dad's Dead will uncover them. And if Neville starts winking in the dark, they can simply say, "I'm sorry, I'm lost right now", and he can help fill in the gaps.

It's a bit like explaining your favourite recipe to someone. It's no good telling them to add chopped fresh coriander at step 12, unless fresh coriander is on the ingredients list at step one.

I often cook from a recipe box where the "correct" ingredients and an easy-to-follow recipe card are delivered to my door. Following these recipe cards has trained me to spot winking in the dark. Each time I reach the end of the cooking process and notice a garlic bulb left in the box or my empty oven turned on, a quick glance at the recipe card shows me why. At no point was I instructed to add the garlic, but I *was* told to preheat my oven for a dish that doesn't require baking – a sign the systems have not been fully tested before they were shared.

My favourite recipes to follow are nice and simple. The more complex the process, the less I'll enjoy cooking it – and the more room for chef error and winking in the dark.

Similarly, Neville explained that he's constantly looking for ways to simplify his processes:

> *"Can the job be done easier? Quicker? Cheaper? Usually, most tasks can be improved and, in some cases, deleted, saving time and money. When we started our internet business, we printed out the order; the packer would take that paper order, find the product, put it in a box, stick the packing note in an envelope, and stick it on the box alongside the address label.*
>
> *I was walking through the warehouse one day, seeing 3,000 envelopes waiting for 3,000 A4 order sheets. I realised that the customer didn't need them as they already had the order information on their computer. It would be easier, quicker, and cheaper to remove the process completely.*
>
> *I saved 28p on each parcel. Multiplied by 3,000 parcels, that's £840 a day, or more than £300,000 a year. I could buy myself a new Ferrari every year thanks to making one process easier, quicker, and cheaper."*

Just because you've always done things a particular way, it doesn't mean that's the best way to do it. Often, time spent documenting your systems and processes (especially if you have to explain or justify them to a third party) uncovers these out-of-date "we've always done it like that" processes that can be removed, making your business more profitable and less time consuming, freeing everyone up to focus on more productive (and profitable) tasks.

A great way to spot this bloat is by walking the floor – as Neville did – with your systems hat on. Spot the systems everywhere. Watch your people at work and ask yourself:

- "What's their system?"

- "Which process are they following?"
- "What should their next step be?"
- "Why are they doing it that way?"
- "Is this process documented anywhere or are they winking in the dark?"

I must repeat the mantra "Where's the system for that?" at least once a day with my team. By parroting "Where's the system?", "Where's the system?", "Where's the system?", I make it clear there are only two reasons things go wrong in our business:

1. The system is broken/wrong and needs to be improved.
2. Someone didn't follow the system.

I'll accept No1, put my Chief Fire Prevention Officer hat on, and get to work improving the system. But No2 is unacceptable. If I'm to exit the day-to-day operations of my business, I need pipelines that work according to a properly designed, deliberate process, instead of relying on me (or anyone) carrying buckets ad hoc. If the system's broken, we'll fix it. But you do not ignore the system.

This is why I constantly walk the virtual corridors of my business, looking for the systems at work, spotting opportunities to make things easier, quicker, and cheaper – as well as hunting for ways to embrace consistency.

For example, say we run a great marketing campaign and want to repeat it a few times a year. Left to their own devices, an individual team member may remember to run the campaign once or maybe twice a year. But with a system that reminds them to send it three times a year every year, as well as capturing the best performing marketing copy, testimonials from happy customers, and analytics showing what works and what doesn't, this campaign not only gets sent more often, but is more impactful, and involves far less work for the team member to simply rinse and repeat.

It's easier, quicker, and cheaper to use a consistent pipeline than it is to carry buckets inconsistently.

THE KING IS DEAD. LONG LIVE THE KING!

In 2019, Plymouth Argyle suffered yet another relegation to the basement division of the English Football League. Manager Derek Adams (who allegedly once described himself as "the best manager outside of the Premier League") was relieved of his duties and replaced with Ryan Lowe, who promised to return the good times to Home Park and "get the place rocking again".

Lowe certainly delivered on that promise, winning promotion at the first attempt with an attack-minded, free-flowing passing game that was beautiful to watch. The following season, Lowe cemented Argyle's foundations in the higher division, while continuing to attract plaudits for his brand of football.

Three months into Ryan Lowe's third year at the club, Argyle found themselves at the top of the table, outperforming far bigger clubs. When Championship side Preston North End were looking for a new manager, they cast glances towards the Pilgrims' progress. I imagine their recruitment process went something like this: "What are little old Plymouth doing at the top of League One? Their manager must be a superstar. Let's have him!" And so, Ryan Lowe swapped Plymouth for Preston.

Having been an Argyle fan for more than three decades now, I'm quite used to managers leaving, but this one felt different. Usually, the manager is sacked because Argyle aren't doing very well. Fans feel that a new man at the top can only be a good thing. Or, the manager is poached by a "bigger" team, because Argyle are punching above their weight. Fans feel devastated because they know this is usually the start of a downward spiral.

When Lowe left for Preston, however, I felt a complete sense of calm. Sure, we'd lost a manager who'd done a really good job for us, but Ryan didn't do it on his own. Throughout his time at Argyle, it was made very clear that the club were building a permanent system that would outlive the current incumbent of the manager's office. When Lowe won the manager of the month award in his final month with the Pilgrims, he was photographed with the entire squad, coaches, admin staff, board of directors, academy prospects, and community leaders, with the simple caption: "It's a team game."

Lowe himself explained: "I'm delighted to win the award, but it is not just recognition for me – it also reflects the work done by my backroom staff, players, our fans and everyone involved at the club throughout the season so far."

When Lowe left, his replacement was announced immediately. And I mean *immediately* – with the new boss unveiled in the same press release confirming Lowe's departure:

> *"Plymouth Argyle Football Club is delighted to announce the appointment of Steven Schumacher as our new First-Team Manager. Schumacher, 37, succeeds outgoing boss Ryan Lowe, who has resigned from his position with the intention of accepting a managerial role elsewhere."*

The King is dead. Long live the King!

Steven Schumacher was no stranger to Argyle fans. He was Ryan Lowe's assistant, and well respected both by the playing staff, and the fanbase, which made him a natural choice to be Lowe's successor. Indeed, this may have been the plan from the very beginning. I chatted to a member of Argyle's board during Lowe's first season with us, expressing that, while the current style of football was the best I had seen in decades, I was worried about what would happen when the manager inevitably leaves. Will the attractive football depart with him?

"Oh no," I was told in no uncertain terms. "This is the Argyle brand of football now. We're building the club around this style, from top to bottom. We're creating a system that will outlive any manager. Ryan's replacement is probably already here."

Argyle have been building this system for years now. Just as I preach to small business owners, Argyle deploy constant, never-ending improvement – leaving the club 1% better each week. They've improved every single aspect of the club; from the training facilities to the youth development, to scouting, players' recovery, data analytics, nutrition, accommodation, corporate hospitality, and stadium improvements.

As I write this, in the last few months alone they have recruited a new head of data analytics, purchased a new training ground, installed a big screen in the stadium, as well as erecting a statue of Jack Leslie, who scored 133 goals for Argyle and would have been the first black player to play for England – until selectors discovered his skin colour.

Crucially, Director of Football Neil Dewsnip remained at the club following Lowe's departure. A former PE teacher, Dewsnip is vastly experienced within the English FA youth setup and has secured fantastic relationships with Premier League clubs, showcasing Plymouth as the destination of choice for the best young players to go to on loan, where they'll benefit from world-class coaching, get plenty of minutes on the pitch, and return to their parent club a much improved player.

Dewsnip even arranged regular Zoom calls between Lowe, Schumacher, and England manager Gareth Southgate.

Everything at Home Park is set up to succeed. A key factor in Argyle's success in recent years (which I hope, given their current trajectory and commitment to constant, never-ending improvement, will continue) is their focus on the *system* as the star. It's the *setup* at Argyle which propelled them to the top of the table, not the godlike genius of one man.

Preston North End did what pretty much every football club does when replacing their manager. They looked at who was doing well at that moment – or did well in the past – and hired them. It's old school thinking that if a club has done well, it must be down to one person – the manager.

With Argyle's system, it's *not* all down to the manager. The manager is simply the frontman. Sure, he's the guy who takes most of the plaudits as well as the criticism. It's his neck on the line if things don't work out. But he's still just one man. When Preston came calling, Argyle effectively sold their frontman (Preston paid a reported £250,000 in compensation), then put those funds to work accelerating their system improvement.

I'm writing this 17 months after the managerial change at Home Park. Lowe's Preston finished mid-table in the Championship, six points outside the playoffs. There's no doubt about it, Preston bought themselves a great manager. But Argyle fans knew that the system was the real star.

Speaking of which, Schumacher's Plymouth Argyle were crowned champions of League One and will compete in the same division as Preston next year.

Schumacher's win percentage since taking over is an astonishing 61.9% (Lowe's by comparison was 42.8%). In recent months, Schumacher has been linked to several high-profile jobs in the Championship and even the Premier League. He's turned them all down so far, but it's only natural that clubs higher up the food chain will cast envious glances towards little old Plymouth and want to poach him.

Steven Schumacher may well prove to be a star manager but long term, the system is the real star.

So who's the star in your business? Is it a bucket-carrying member of staff? Is it you? Or is it a world class system? What happens if someone poaches your star salesperson or copies your best performing marketing pillar? Well, if the system is the star in your business, then they may have your star salesperson, but they won't have the system that made them a star. And sure, they could copy your marketing, but they won't have the system which maximises the ROI from it.

The system is the star. But where does the system start?

SYSTEM ASSETS FOR SYSTEM ADDICTS

In *Evergreen Assets*, I highlighted the six asset classes which are essential for every small business:

1. Lead Assets – to make your phone ring.
2. Nurture Assets – to make sure prospects take your call.
3. Sales Assets – to make the till ring.
4. Fulfilment Assets – to make sure the cash stays in the till.
5. Admin Assets – to make everything run like clockwork.
6. Viral Assets – to make one customer tell another... and another... and another...

To start systemising your business, begin by capturing the "big picture" – the macro information detailing how to run the business using each asset class as a guide.

Imagine you've been suddenly called away for a couple of weeks. You've got 30 minutes to tell me how to run your business and then your livelihood is in *my* hands for the next few weeks. Will you spend this next half hour telling me how to reconcile line items on your cloud accounting software or what to do in the event of a HMRC audit?

I hope not! Hopefully, you'll tell me how to ensure the phone keeps ringing with new leads. You'll let me know how you'd like me to treat prospects, give me some basic training on what sells and how to sell it. You'll show me how to ensure customers are satisfied and make sure everything ticks over until your return. In other words, you'll give me the headlines – the important stuff.

For some reason though, most small business owners try to systemise their business by documenting every little thing. They don't even start *using* the systems until everything's documented. I include myself in that sweeping statement by the way. One of my previous attempts to exit the business included putting together a "bible" of systems and processes. Jason and I spent the best part of six months putting everything together in one place.

Our bible was a thing of beauty – 68 pages covering everything you ever wanted to know about running our business. Well actually, that's not strictly true. It was more like three pages covering everything you ever wanted to know about running our business and 65 pages of the things we *thought* were important. I've just dug it out. It's the first time it's seen daylight in seven years. Six months to create and then ignored for seven years. Slow hand clap, John!

No one wants a 68-page manual. So give them a one-page cheat-sheet instead. Give them the headlines and tell them what matters most. Start with the big picture items first – those processes that your business simply could not operate without. They tend to be the two or three processes that power each of the six asset classes – lead generation, nurturing prospects, making sales, product/service fulfilment, admin, and generating referrals and recommendations.

THE EVERGREEN FLYWHEEL

Earlier, *Good to Great* author Jim Collins helped us get the right people on our bus, the wrong people off the bus, and the right people in the right seats. Now, Jim is going to help us create a flywheel based on his belief that great businesses are built on the momentum generated by thousands of tiny actions rather than grand step-changes:

> *"There's no single defining action. No grand program, no single killer innovation, no solitary lucky break, no miracle moment. Rather it feels like turning a giant, heavy flywheel. Pushing with great effort, you get the flywheel to inch forward. You keep pushing and with persistent effort, you get the flywheel to complete one entire turn. You don't stop. You keep pushing. The flywheel moves a bit faster. Two turns... then four... then eight... the flywheel builds momentum... sixteen... thirty-two... moving faster... a thousand... ten thousand... a hundred thousand...*
>
> *Each turn builds upon previous work as you make a series of good decisions, supremely well executed, that compound one upon another. That is how you build greatness."*

In *Turning The Flywheel*, Collins demonstrates how huge companies such as Amazon, Intel, and Vanguard (as well as tiny enterprises such as health clinics, music festivals and schools) all used flywheels to harness the power of strategic compounding.

Regular readers of my work will know I'm a Warren Buffett fanboy and, like most Buffett-heads, a devout worshipper at the altar of compounding. Strategic compounding enables you to bake momentum and exponential growth into your business model.

Amazon's flywheel was described in Brad Stone's *The Everything Store*: "Bezos and his lieutenants sketched their own virtuous cycle, which they believed powered their business. It went something like this: Lower prices led to more customer visits. More customers increased the volume of sales and attracted more commission-paying third-party sellers to the site. That allowed Amazon to get more out of fixed costs like the fulfilment centers and the servers needed to run the website. This greater efficiency then enabled it to lower prices further. Feed any part of this flywheel, they reasoned, and it should accelerate the loop."

Founder Jeff Bezos referred to Amazon's flywheel as their "secret sauce". How on Earth can a business with, at the time of writing, more than 1.6million employees, selling 350million different items to 310million customers all over the planet, possibly be powered by such a simple five-step model?

The answer is just as simple: this flywheel is Amazon's high-level strategy for success. It's the big picture stuff – the macro. There may be hundreds or even thousands of micro tactics which enable Amazon to offer lower prices or increase visits to the website. But rather than getting lost in the details, Bezos wants his team to remember what matters most – *why* they're implementing these tactics. I began this section by telling you that the flywheel concept was based on "the momentum generated by thousands of tiny actions". Well, it's not about taking thousands of *different* actions. Rather, it's actually about the momentum generated by *repeating* a small number of actions thousands of times.

The more moving parts your business has, the more important it is not to lose focus on what matters most – the flywheel that powers your business.

Jim Collins offers the following advice on how to create your flywheel:

1. Create a list of significant replicable successes your enterprise has achieved. This should include new initiatives and offerings that have far exceeded expectations.
2. Compile a list of failures and disappointments. This should include new initiatives and offerings by your enterprise that have failed outright or fell below expectations.

3. Compare the successes to the disappointments and ask 'What do these successes and disappointments tell us about the possible components of our flywheel?'.
4. Using the components you've identified (keeping it to four to six), sketch the flywheel. Where does the flywheel start – what's the top of the loop? What follows next? And next after that? You should be able to explain *why* each component follows from the previous component. Outline the path back to the top of the loop. You should be able to explain how this loop cycles back upon itself to accelerate momentum.
5. If you have more than six components, you're making it too complicated; consolidate and simplify to capture the essence of the flywheel.
6. Test the flywheel against your list of successes and disappointments. Does your empirical experience validate it? Tweak the diagram until you can explain your biggest replicable successes as outcomes arising directly from the flywheel, and your biggest disappointments as failures to execute or adhere to the flywheel.

It's worth taking a few minutes to sit with some blank paper right now and start sketching your flywheel (there's also a template in the resources section). It's probably been a long time since you thought of your business in such simple, macro-level terms as a five or six-step process. But it's really powerful when you do.

I use the following flywheels in my businesses.

My info-marketing business flywheel:

First and foremost, we identify information or data that gives our clients an edge over the general public. We then use that data to create marketable systems and services.

Next, we sell those services using proven direct response marketing strategies, enabling us to focus on our "Retention First" strategy of prioritising existing customers over new ones. If we successfully retain enough customers, we generate surplus profit, which we reinvest into research and development, helping us discover our next data-driven advantage, thus closing the loop.

Around and around we go. Can you see how one step inevitably leads to the next? If we use data to find an edge, the systems create themselves. If we create really good systems, they're easy to market. And if our marketing is firing on all cylinders, we have more customers to retain, which gives us more money to invest in finding the next edge.

My coaching business flywheel:

Again, notice how each component on the flywheel is an almost inevitable consequence of the previous one.

The more books I write, the more books I can sell. The more books I sell, the more readers I can build relationships with. The better I nurture relationships with readers, the more people will be attracted to the One Percent Club. The more people who join the club, the more members I can deliver for. And the more One Percenters who stay with me for years, the more I can focus on my own personal development, staying true to my own core value of constant, never-ending improvement.

This gives me more knowledge, expertise, and content, which I can share by writing even more books – and round we go again!

Best of all, I can direct my efforts to any point of the flywheel and the whole thing will speed up. In the last 12 months, I've invested heavily in the Retention First component, step five on my flywheel. To start with, I bought three hospitality season tickets in the posh seats at Home Park, for myself, my business partner Jason and a third seat, which we use to invite a One Percenter to come and spend six hours picking our brains, while being wined, dined, and enjoying the best seats in the house, watching the best football club in the world (that's Plymouth Argyle, for the avoidance of doubt).

Next, I overhauled our members' website, soliciting (as well as implementing) feedback from members about what they liked, loved and hated about the group. I even spent several months locked away in my office writing another book *just* for One Percenters (that's right, it's not publicly available. You can't buy a copy for love nor money. The only way to get one is to join the One Percent Club).

What happened as a result of all this work on step five of my flywheel? Well, One Percenters now stay with us for longer, enabling me to invest more heavily in my personal development, giving me the time (and knowledge) to write more books like this. Which, of course, means I sell more books, befriend more readers, and therefore welcome more people into the One Percent Club.

Yes, you read that correctly – because I worked on step five of my flywheel, I see better results from step four. That's strategic compounding at work, my friend.

BUT MY BUSINESS IS FAR MORE COMPLICATED THAN THAT!

I know what you're thinking: "But John, my business is more complicated than that. You're massively oversimplifying things. There's no way my business runs on five or six key components."

Well, let me remind you that Amazon's "secret sauce" flywheel contained just five:

1. Lower prices on more offerings.
2. Increase customer visits.
3. Attract third-party sellers.
4. Expand the store, extend distribution.
5. Grow revenues per fixed cost.

If five high-level principles are good enough to build a trillion dollar company, with 1.6million employees and hundreds of millions of customers, then four to six should be plenty for your small business.

One Percenter Stephen Gibbens is an accountant, who specialises in working closely with tech start-ups which want to make a positive impact on the world. He's also a fellow convert to the flywheel concept. Stephen sent me this proposed flywheel:

1. Find the best start-ups from university, through relationships with spin-out people and advisors/angels. We only choose to work with the best start-ups but need to discover the best ways to find those. Help them to bootstrap through the development stage by obtaining every available grant, R&D tax credits and not wasting money. Only small pre-seed amounts raised as equity at this stage.
2. Teach them best practice from other more experienced start-ups and our own experience. Form a community/club of start-ups that others desire to be in.

3. Give each client our full attention so that we are always up to date with how they are doing and can help them adjust/pivot if need be and find appropriate help for them when needed. Introduce them to other advisors who provide complementary services to our own.
4. Help them raise investment at as late a stage as they can, to maximise their valuation. (Normally once there is market interest, but before sales have *really* taken off, the stage where money is needed for marketing and systemising operations). Help them build a viable plan and do financial forecasts for them.
5. Get investors to know that our companies are good ones to invest in based on the track record of previous clients. Maintain close relationships with investors to let them know what opportunities are upcoming, when our clients are looking to raise finance, and how much is needed. Get to know what sort of client appeals to each investor.
6. Ensure founders succeed, and should they sell/exit, encourage them to become mentors to new clients or investors in new clients or to launch a new start-up themselves. Back to the beginning again!

Now, I haven't demonstrated Stephen's flywheel with a diagram for the same reason I encouraged him to think again – it's too complicated. Remember, the flywheel is a high-level, key principles document.

Yes, Stephen needs to know exactly what "the best start-ups" look like and that he will help them bootstrap with the assistance of grants, research & development tax credits, and a frugality that won't come naturally to a young excitable businessperson with a big pile of fresh investment cash. But for the sake of simplicity, this first component on Stephen's flywheel could be summed up as simply: "Find the best tech start-ups."

Here's a far simpler version of Stephen's flywheel (I've added a little explanation in brackets to each principle just to add context, as you won't be familiar with Stephen's business):

1. Find the best tech start-ups. (Find the best purposeful tech company start-ups through Stephen's network of contacts).
2. Get them investor ready. (Make their cash stretch as far as possible through hands-on help from Stephen's team with 20 years' tech experience accessing grants/R&D tax credits, etc).
3. Help them raise seed investment. (Provide assistance with projections, Enterprise Investment Scheme applications, etc).
4. Expand their network. (Introduce them to the rest of Stephen's start-up community and other key contacts who can help them scale).
5. Raise "Series A" investment. (Help them raise further investment, achieve initial sales, and implement appropriate systems to support growth at scale).
6. Expand our network. (Encourage referrals from successful clients and investors who know Stephen's firm is well-placed to help the best purposeful tech company start-ups and tech investors achieve their goals).

With a simpler flywheel, you can better see how each component is actually the logical next step from the successful execution of the previous one:

- If Stephen finds the best tech start-ups, they'll be more likely to be investor ready.
- If he makes them investor ready, they'll be able to raise seed investment.
- Once they raise seed money, they'll want to spend that money wisely with people and companies who can help them scale, growing their network.

- As their network expands, they will be better placed for Series A investment.
- If they reach this milestone, they should be in a position to be a valuable asset to Stephen's network.

And, of course, if Stephen has successful tech start-up entrepreneurs and investors in his network, then he should be able to find the best tech start-ups more easily, taking us back around the flywheel again, adding ever more momentum to Stephen's business.

Now it fits into a diagram.

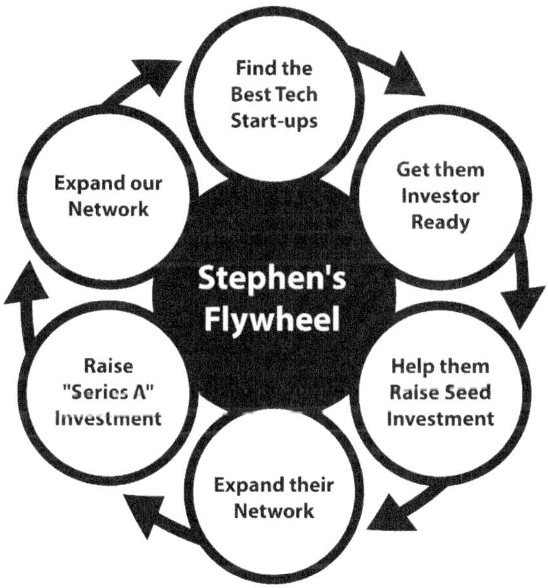

Just like your core values, your flywheel should be short and snappy enough to paint on the walls if you wanted. However, just like your core values, it must also be lived and breathed. Of course, on a micro level, your business *is* more complicated than a simple five or six-step process. But at the macro level, it really isn't. The flywheel captures the biggest, most essential, irreplaceable cogs in your machine. As you stop carrying buckets and start building pipelines, the flywheel represents the key milestones that matter most – cross this valley; climb that mountain; serve this village. It doesn't list every twist and turn or every nut and bolt.

THE FLYWHEEL WITHIN THE FLYWHEEL

Having captured the macro flywheel, your team still needs to know how to bring the rubber to the road and actually execute the micro – the huge number of processes that need to happen every day to keep your business ticking.

Imagine your goal is to climb a mountain range, which is several days' hike away. First, you look up, scan the horizon, and ensure that the mountains are in sight – that you're heading in the right direction. Still looking up at the big picture, you might scan for some waypoints – a village, a stream, a church. You'd get the first of these in your sights, plot a course there, and then look down.

Why look down rather than continuing to focus on the goal in the distance? Because if you don't, you'll trip over rocks or fall in a pothole. You need to navigate the small obstacles in your immediate path, while remaining on course for the next waypoint. In doing so, you'll be on course for the overarching goal – the mountain on the horizon.

It's the same with your systems. You need to ensure that your team knows what the overarching goal is, as well as the waypoints that will keep them on track to achieve that goal. Once they understand that, however, it's imperative they look down and focus on the micro – the processes that will ensure they reach the next macro milestone without tripping and falling on their face.

With your main flywheel, you've identified the mountain on your horizon, as well as the milestones en route. To plot a course to each milestone, you can simply create another flywheel one level below your macro goal. A flywheel within a flywheel if you will.

Remember Amazon's flywheel? The first component was: "Lower prices on more offerings." So, how does Amazon achieve that? Well, let's create a flywheel within a flywheel. Once again, there are hundreds of micro tactics that Amazon could deploy to achieve lower prices on more offerings, but we're looking for the five or six significant replicable successes, where each step is an inevitable consequence of the preceding action, and which leverages strategic compounding to make achieving the goal inevitable.

1. Encourage price competition.
2. Own brand products.
3. Be frugal.
4. High turnover of stock.
5. Data-led pricing.

For clarity's sake, this isn't an official Amazon flywheel, rather, it's my interpretation of how they *might* achieve that first milestone on their macro flywheel of "lower prices on more offerings".

For me, the first step on this second-tier flywheel is encouraging price competition. Having dozens (or in some cases hundreds) of third-party sellers for each individual item, and giving the lowest prices priority at the top of their algorithm, ensures that everyone on the platform knows that if you want to sell on Amazon, you have to be competitive on price.

Next are own-brand products. A great way that Amazon ensures price competition is to avoid paying any margin whatsoever to third-party sellers by creating the products themselves. This gives them more margin, which they could then forsake in order to create loss-leaders (items priced to break even, or lose money, to bring customers into the store, where they will purchase higher margin items).

This naturally leads to step three on the flywheel – an obsession with frugality, keeping overheads low and reducing margins. Amazon knows how to squeeze every last ounce of margin out of each product. And despite being a trillion-dollar company, Amazon is ruthlessly frugal and never wastes money.

To this day, Amazon's offices are full of "door-desks", a money saving tactic Jeff Bezos discovered in 1995.

"We happened to be across the street from a Home Depot," explained Nico Lovejoy, who was Amazon's fifth ever employee. "Jeff looked at desks for sale and looked at doors for sale, and the doors were a lot cheaper, so he decided to buy a door and put some legs on it."

Decades later, Amazon employees continue to work on modern versions of the original door-desk.

By keeping overheads and margins low, Amazon ensures a high turnover of stock, reducing the amount of perishable items spoiling or low-demand items gathering dust on stockroom shelves for months on end, tying up valuable cash.

Finally, this high turnover of stock gives Amazon a tremendous amount of data about the peaks and troughs of supply and demand, which is then used to adjust prices dynamically.

Amazon tweaks product prices 2.5million times a day, meaning an average product's price will change about once every ten minutes. Of course, this data is then used to take us back around the flywheel once more to the first step of encouraging price competition.

The faster this second-tier flywheel turns, the better the "Lower prices on more offerings" component of Amazon's main flywheel will perform. This doesn't just work for trillion dollar companies like Amazon. Remember my coaching business's flywheel?

Write books > Sell books > Reader Relationships > One Percent Club > Retention First > Constant, Never-Ending Improvement.

Each of those six macro components can be drilled down further, with a second-tier flywheel detailing the key steps to achieve the macro goal.

Here's my second-tier flywheel for "Reader Relationships":

There may come a day when I get so much fan mail that this becomes impossible. Until then, replying to every reader who gets in touch *really* matters to me. The way I see it, if someone has invested several hours reading one of my books and then takes a few more minutes to get in touch with me, then the least I can do is take a minute or two to reply.

Next, I have to be genuine. What do I mean by that? Well, I've reached out personally to authors I respect, whose books have helped me, and received either disappointing stock replies or a thinly veiled advert for their coaching platform, mastermind group or next book. It's clear that I'm just another sale to them. I genuinely care about my readers' success. I want you to take the information in my books and use it to make *your* life better.

Third stop on the Reader Relationships flywheel is to help readers connect the dots between the words in my books and the reality of their life. To show them what I think *their* next step should be, whether that's recommending their next read, explaining a concept in more detail or giving my opinion on the best path for them to achieve their goals.

Next, I send weekly emails. I've written in far more detail, in both *Routine Machine* and *Evergreen Assets*, about the amazing power of sending a weekly email that doesn't sell anything. It's a pure relationship builder. At the time of writing, I've created 187 weekly emails and automated them to be delivered to new subscribers every Wednesday lunchtime for the 187 weeks. If you'd like to start getting them (they're free and I promise they don't try to sell you *anything*!), you can do so via my website: www.bigidea.co.uk.

Finally, I want to keep the conversation going. I ask a lot of open-ended questions in my weekly emails, encouraging readers to hit reply and answer them, which takes me back to the first step of the flywheel, where I reply once more, being genuine, and helping them connect the dots again.

MY 136TH MISTAKE

Having identified the mountain on the horizon (our main flywheel) and the key milestones along the way (the second-tier flywheels), we can now begin to look down even more, plotting the micro steps that will take us to that first milestone. It's time to start thinking about *all* the processes that need to be followed.

I made many mistakes when systemising my business. My 136th mistake was trying to create all the systems myself, including every micro process. This seemed logical at first. After all, who better to know how to run a business than the business owner? Well, if systems are to run my business and my team are to run the systems then, actually, my team should capture the processes because they're on the front line day-in, day-out.

Sure, I could create a perfect, 17-step process which completely optimises the procedure and captures the "right" way to do it (the way *I* would do it). But the person actually doing the job knows a far simpler five-step process which takes half the time and gets 98% of the output.

When systems are created by the people who will actually run those systems, they're more likely to be used. Handing an experienced member of staff a brand new "correct way to do your job" process and expecting them to use it is naive. But if you ask them to document their "right way", it's far more likely to be adhered to consistently. And consistency is our priority.

What's the best diet? The one you stick to.

What's the best exercise routine? The one you do regularly.

What's the best system? The one that gets used.

Consistency trumps perfection every time.

Us business owners crave perfection. We seek Dolly the Sheep clones of ourselves, wishing everyone else thought and acted exactly as we would. But that's simply not realistic. And if we're ever to exit the firefighting, bucket-carrying, so-called-perfection that is running our business, then we need to build a *consistent* pipeline – even if it's not perfect.

With the benefit of hindsight, here's how I would systemise my business today, avoiding repeating mistake No136. I would design the main flywheel for the business myself. This is top-level strategy and you don't want decision by committee on your primary strategy. As you start to filter down through the process, however, the more you'll benefit from the involvement of the people who will be doing the work.

Therefore, I would involve key members of my team in the creation of the second-tier flywheels. This should be a collaborative effort, between me as the pipeline designer and my head of department(s). These people may not know or understand the entire business, but will be experts in the five or six components on their second-tier flywheel. Together, we'll bring the rubber to the road – to stay on track with the main flywheel, while leveraging departmental expertise to reverse-engineer how to achieve each component.

Then, as we drill down further to the individual processes, ideally, I wouldn't be involved whatsoever. Yep, that's right. I would delegate this entirely to the team/person who will be following the process. Any interference from me will be just that – interference. Meddling for the sake of it. Trying to micro-manage every aspect of your business will end in disaster. There's a reason they don't hand out micro-manager of the month awards.

Ask yourself this: If all your second-tier flywheels are working nicely, causing your main flywheel to accelerate and work efficiently without you, do you *really* care how each individual process is achieved? Now, I'm a micro-manager at heart, so if you're stressing about letting go right now, I get it. I understand. Many times I've seen an email my team has sent to customers and cringed because I spotted a typo or missed opportunity. I've had to reprogram my muscle memory to not react to every little thing, virtually sitting on my hands and biting my lip at the same time.

I know I should be focused on how the pipeline is functioning, rather than critiquing how the buckets are being carried, but it is very difficult to change the habit of a lifetime and let go. And yet, let go we must. There are far more micro processes in your business than there are big picture flywheels. If you focus on the micro, your day will be full of micro-management and you'll have no capacity to improve the macro, which is what really matters.

My advice is this: coach your team hard on the macro and soft on the micro. By all means give them the hairdryer treatment if they're deviating from your vision and values, ignoring your decision-making framework or sabotaging your flywheel. But go easy on them if they're deviating slightly on the micro processes. Coach soft, giving them permission to customise and tweak the processes, making them their own – but coach hard and insist on having processes that are followed consistently.

You design the main flywheel. You design the second-tier flywheels (with help from your department heads). Then, let go and trust your team to design the individual processes they will (or perhaps already do) use to achieve the key flywheel elements. Your job is to remain at the big picture level, focusing on the macro, while your team at the coal face looks after the micro.

START WHERE YOU ARE, NOT WHERE YOU WANT TO BE

Where should you keep your system documents? Should you create an online bible? A physical manual? Plaster notices all over the walls?

Personally, I use a combination of Task Management Software (TMS) and Google Docs. I use the TMS to remind team members when to do a particular task and link to the Google Doc which shows how to do the task. This separates the two:

1. The requirement to do the task.
2. How to correctly do the task.

An experienced member of staff should only need No1 – the regular reminder to do a certain task when it needs doing. A simple nudge to call a few lapsed customers each week, a monthly task to chase outstanding invoices, a quarterly reminder to run a stock check. They probably already know how to do each of these tasks, so it's far more important that they are reminded *to* do it in the first place.

We rinse and repeat a handful of evergreen marketing campaigns three times a year and, as much of the marketing copy is reused, it's quite a simple task to complete and provides a fantastic ROI. When chatting with our marketing department recently, though, I asked when we last sent this campaign. "Erm, I think it was a couple of months ago."

I checked and it was *six* months ago. This is a campaign that doesn't take much time, the heavy lifting has already been done and is something we want to repeat every four months, and yet it's been gathering dust for the past six months, because – well, why do you think?

Yep, you've guessed it. My catchphrase came out again: "Where's the system for this campaign?" I already knew the answer of course because there wasn't one. Which was how an easy-to-do, high-ROI marketing campaign was forgotten.

By the way, I've just checked in our TMS and there is now a system for this campaign. It's scheduled to go out soon and to automatically repeat every four months. The TMS system also contains links to all the email copy and results from the last time we sent this campaign, making it even easier for us to simply copy, paste and send next time.

Most small businesses aren't systemised. Why not? Because the business owners are petrified at the scale of the job. They think they need to document every single process in precise detail before running those systems. If they do start systemising, they soon get overwhelmed. Facing months of pushing treacle uphill, they eventually take the easy way out and go back to carrying their own buckets.

There's great value in starting by documenting the systems you already have rather than the systems you want to have. Remember, our goal is consistency, not perfection. Consistency is a superpower and consistency should be your primary objective when documenting your systems. Getting what you're currently doing *most* of the time to happen *all* of the time is the lowest hanging fruit. That one system, for example, to ensure our marketing campaign happens every four months without fail, as opposed to three times a year if we remember (and twice if we don't) pays for itself many times over.

This is another good reason why you, dear business owner, should leave documenting the processes well alone. Sure, you know what the perfect process looks like. But that's the problem – you'd document the perfect process. Flawless in every one of its 23 pieces of detail. Once again, the best process is the one that gets followed consistently. You can always improve the process later (and if you're like me, there's a system for doing that, too). But, for now, let's get the bloody thing used first.

Again, think of your processes as two steps: when to do it, and how to do it. Task Management Software manages the "when" and links to the "how".

Say I want to capture our process for rebilling failed payments. What's the first thing I should document? That's right – nothing! As the business owner, I'm not supposed to be documenting any micro processes. Instead, I'll ask my head of customer service to capture what she currently does and how often she feels this task should be performed.

"It's best if we can keep on top of it, while the failed payments are fresh in customer's minds," she explains. "Otherwise, they forget that they even tried to buy from us. I think we should do it three times a week."

A quick look in the logs tells us that, without a system, this task is currently performed just once a week on average and is sometimes neglected for as long as three weeks. Again, let's get some consistency before we try and optimise the process.

Next, I'll ask them to document the how-to process of retrying the payments; asking them to create a Google Doc with a step-by-step written process, including everything you would need in order to complete the task. This includes login information and common problems or issues to watch out for. If there are a lot of moving parts that require further explanation then it's often easier for the person capturing the process, (as well as the person following the process) to record a video.

We use Loom for this, which records your screen and webcam at the same time, meaning you can record what you're doing and narrate. At any point, the person following can pause the video and check their screen looks like that of the instructor. If it doesn't, they can rewind and see where they went wrong (or where your process needs updating).

You may get some kickback from one or more of your team. "Why am I wasting my time documenting all these processes, when it's only me who does this work and I already know how the process works?" Well, they make a valid point – until they either call in sick one day or leave forever. If they don't show up to carry the buckets for whatever reason, you need to train someone else in the how-to, because it was never captured. Watch your "Oh Shit-o-meter" go to 11 on that day!

I have a small team in which most roles are performed by an individual. So when that person is on holiday, off sick or leaves the company, someone else has to be able to cover a job that they very rarely do. For example, Luke sends a daily email to our members. It's quite a complex email, with various information being pulled in from multiple sources and all weaved together in a particular format. It has to be sent by 9am each morning as it contains time-sensitive information.

If Luke wants to book a two-week holiday, he needs this process documented so that one of his colleagues can send the email each day while he's on leave. Luke did a sterling job of capturing the process in a step-by-step text format, also recording a Loom video of himself executing the process as a visual aid.

Hey presto! For two weeks, Sian, another member of our team, successfully collated and sent this email and our members didn't notice any disruption. A few months later, Luke booked a long weekend away, and this time Mel covered for him – following the same process that Sian had. Once again, we got the same result. Consistency.

Of course, experienced members of staff running the same process again and again won't need to see the "how to". But, crucially, by marking the task as complete in the Task Management Software, they are declaring that they have done it to the standard contained in the "how to" (as documented by themselves).

Systems make things easier for your team in the long run, save them time and enable them to have time off without all the work waiting for them on their return. Plus, the more consistency you can harness, the more predictable your revenue streams will be, which of course means more money for pay reviews and bonuses.

But what if you're the only person in your business? This is the classic self-employed conundrum – you're too busy carrying buckets to build pipelines. You're busy carrying buckets today because you didn't start a pipeline yesterday. So start now. Make a list of the tasks that someone could do instead of you. Record yourself on Loom performing that task, narrating as you go. Then put that video into your TMS and decide how often that task should be repeated. This may add a few minutes to each task but it's one more process logged forever (almost). One more piece of the pipeline assembled.

Some people employ a personal assistant to follow them around, capturing processes on their behalf. You could hire a virtual assistant to do the same by sharing your screen online. Task them with documenting all of your processes; interviewing you at regular intervals to discover what you've done, how you've done it, and how someone else can (and eventually will) do it in the future. They can even be a guinea pig, testing your processes exactly as documented and seeing whether they get the same results as you.

It's vital that other people are able to accurately replicate your results by following the steps laid out in the documented processes. If a new hire can't walk in off the street, sit down at a computer, and follow our process for rebilling failed card payments, then we've gone wrong somewhere. We've either made the process too complicated to follow or we've been "winking in the dark" again, assuming that everyone else knows what we're doing without telling them.

Choosing to systemise is not a "one and done" process, however. You have to choose to become a systems-centric business. You have to develop a systems mindset and see the world in systems. You'll know when you truly have a systems mindset because you'll start noticing them everywhere, not just in your business, but in other people's. And you'll really notice their absence, adopting my catchphrase: "Where's your system for that?"

THE FUCKING CHEESE IS NOT FUCKING RIGHT!

I feel sorry for my team.

I was once asked my greatest weakness. I answered in less than a tenth of a second: "Other people." Other people are like my kryptonite. My wife even bought me a T-shirt which read: "Caution: Doesn't play well with others!" This is why I'm a terrible manager. Rousing the troops with a stirring speech just doesn't come naturally to me. You see, I'm not a people person. Nor am I a motivator. I'm incredibly self-motivated, so I expect others to be, as well. I work best locked away in my home office alone. Undistracted. Uninterrupted. Uncontactable.

This is why I lean heavily on my vision and values, ensuring my team has access to my decision-making framework, as well as the systems they need to run the business without me.

And that all works swimmingly as long as my vision and values are honoured, my decision-making frameworks followed, and the systems actually used. Once, I noticed I was starting to put out small fires in the day-to-day running of the business once more. Marketing emails weren't being sent on time. Our website hadn't been updated in months. Paid members were complaining they didn't have access to the service they were paying for while others were getting free access to services they weren't paying for.

I didn't understand what was going on. After all, we had systems to make sure this didn't happen. Those systems were created based on my decision-making framework and were the cornerstone of one of our main values, which was communicated with team members on day one of joining the team and repeated cult-like on a weekly basis: "We're a systems-run company. The systems run the business and our people run the systems."

The problem was, apart from myself, no one else was actually following the system. When I looked at my to-do list in our TMS (where all of our systems live), I saw a handful of overdue tasks and dozens of upcoming tasks lined up for the next few weeks. By comparison, when I looked at my team's to-do lists, I saw hundreds of overdue tasks dating back more than 18 months. More worryingly, everyone else had zero tasks due in the coming weeks despite a major launch being imminent, as well as regular weekly and monthly routines which are mission-critical for the company's success.

Every time I talked about being "systems-run", my team would smile and nod. They'd smile and agree with me wholeheartedly that, of course, the systems *were* running the business. They'd nod – yes, they *were* running the systems. They'd smile. They'd nod. And then they'd do their own thing. They'd wing it. They'd do whatever they felt like in the moment.

Of course, they knew exactly what they were doing, why they'd done it, and what was going to happen next but no one else had a Scooby-Doo. They were winking in the dark.

Why do I get so irate about it? Because it's part of our values. We can't be a "systems-run company" if I'm the only person in the company following the bloody system. I felt as if I was preaching to the choir each week, only to find that my preaching was falling on deaf ears, while they smiled and nodded.

The value of being a systems-run company is only a competitive advantage if the value is actually lived and breathed, rather than smiled and nodded. This is why I coach my team hard on strategy like this. I'm still soft on tactics – they're free to decide what the step-by-step process looks like for each system – but there will be a system, it will be part of the company system, and it must be used. That's non-negotiable.

So I lost my temper and "coached hard", ranting for several minutes about the importance of systems. I explained that consistency was supposed to be our superpower. I signposted mistakes that had been made and revenue lost simply due to established systems not being followed. The hairdryer came out:

> *"Why did we only send our best performing marketing campaign twice last year, rather than the three times we're supposed to?"*
>
> *"You're all winging it – making it up as you go along! And when you're not winging it, you're winking in the dark!"*

> *"What happens when you leave the company with your system still in your head? Your system leaves with you!"*
>
> *"It's a good job I don't pay you only when I remember to, plucking the figures out of the air and guessing what your bank details are, isn't it? No – I've got a system for paying you!"*

Finally, I asked the tough question of each and every one of them: "If we're a systems-run company, why aren't you following the system?"

The answers I received were illuminating:

> *"I don't need the system; I just write everything down."*
>
> *"I do use systems, they're just in my head."*
>
> *"I use my own spreadsheet."*
>
> *"I got overwhelmed with too many processes, so when I fell behind, the overwhelm compounded, and I stopped using the system completely."*
>
> *"I don't use it because other people don't either."*

My team wasn't deliberately sabotaging my attempts to be systems-run. The systems I designed were too complicated for them. We're a small team running a small business and I tried to systemise every tiny aspect of the business – every customer contact, each email that was sent, every single process.

So, I set to work simplifying the systems. Encouraging the team to create their own, rather than be dictated to from above, and focusing primarily on the "immovable objects" first – the key components on their respective department's flywheel. Once we had some simpler systems captured, I realised we now needed a simple system to ensure our systems were being used.

How would you deal with your team ignoring your systems? And how do you ensure they get the message in a way that sticks with them? Chefs Marco Pierre White and Heston Blumenthal have very different approaches. Upon spotting a cheese trolley containing a piece of cheese that was two-thirds too small, Marco Pierre White stopped his maître d' Nicolas in his tracks:

"Where are you going with that, Nicolas?"

"I am taking it to table 12, Marco."

"No. No, no, no, no, fuck no!"

"Sorry, Marco."

"Not right, Nicolas, not correct. The fucking cheese is not fucking right!"

"Sorry Marco."

Marco picks up the first bit of cheese – "Not right!" – and with all his might, threw it at the wall, where it stuck to the tiles. He then picked up the second bit of cheese and launched that one too: "Not right!"

One after another, each piece of Brie, Camembert and Stilton was propelled at the kitchen wall – "Not right!", "Not right!", "Not fucking right!" – where they remained steadfastly stuck to the tiles. Nicolas and a few kitchen porters raced over to clean the cheesy mess up.

"Leave them there! Fucking leave them there all fucking night! No one's allowed to touch them!". Marco insisted the cheese remain on the wall for the duration of that evening's service, so his team would see the sticky mess each time they entered the kitchen, as a physical reminder to follow the system.

By contrast, Chris Young, former head chef at The Fat Duck, describes how Heston Blumenthal had a similar lasting effect without uttering a single f-bomb, or lobbing any cheese:

> *"I sent these quail jellies out knowing they weren't perfect. Those things came back like a boomerang. Heston flew around the corner with them in his hand and just said, 'Chris'.*
>
> *He looks at me, then looks at the dish. Back at me, and back at the dish. I just remember the withering look that said, 'If you ever try anything like that again, don't bother showing up'."*

So how did *I* get my systems followed? Well, I didn't have any cheese to throw at the wall and I couldn't rely on my withering looks. Instead, someone suggested I try the "peer traffic light" technique – a simple yet quickly effective way to gain compliance, spot problems early, and understand why systems aren't being followed. We began to display two numbers (in one of three colours) next to each team member's name on our weekly metrics meeting scorecard:

1. The number of overdue tasks (0-1 is green, 2-3 is amber, 4+ is red).
2. The number of tasks due in the next 14 days (4+ is green, 2-3 is amber, 0-1 is red).

This simple red-amber-green traffic light system suddenly makes it visible (to everyone) who is smiling and nodding, and who's living and breathing the "systems-run" value. We know exactly who's winking in the dark and who's winging it. The traffic light system alerts the entire team to two early warning signs that someone isn't following the system:

1. They're not completing tasks that are due (at least not via the system).
2. They're not adding upcoming tasks to the system.

The first week we displayed the numbers, I had zero tasks outstanding and 28 tasks coming up in the next two weeks. By contrast, the rest of the team averaged 25 tasks outstanding and one upcoming task.

These polar opposites were a clear indication that they weren't using the system. One week later, however, all but one team member had cleared their outstanding tasks and started to add jobs for the coming weeks and months.

A private conversation with the straggler (again, praise in public, shame in private) uncovered the reason they weren't using the system and enabled us to reinforce the importance of systems and deal with the issue, allowing them to customise the system for their role, again coaching hard on the strategy (of being systems-run), but soft on the tactics of what those systems look like.

Where there's persistent red, this clearly demonstrates an area that needs attention. If it's a particular system that keeps flashing red, that system may need work (it may need to be made simpler or you may need to provide more training or support). If it's a particular team member drowning in red, they may be silently crying out for help. Having the clear visual traffic light system means you can give them support, training or buddy them up with another who is constantly green. At the very least, it enables you to do two things that I failed to do for 18 months:

1. Notice that people aren't following the system.
2. Find out why and do something about it.

Within a few weeks of showing the traffic light scores in our metrics meetings, a sea of red turned to an ocean of green. What gets measured (and displayed publicly to your peers), gets improved. No one wants to see their name next to a red score and all want to be green like their "better" peers.

Of course, the real magic happens when you can spend your time improving your systems and compounding your gains, rather than chasing your tail trying to achieve compliance.

HOW I PLUGGED A LEAKY BUCKET WITH A PINK FLAMINGO

You need to dig those flywheels out again – both your main and second-tier ones – because we're going to score them all.

On your main flywheel, give each component a mark out of ten based on your current performance in that area. If, for example, you have six components on your flywheel and you score them 7, 9, 7, 8, 3 and 6, it's clear which element of your current systems isn't firing on all cylinders. Next, take a look at the second-tier flywheel for the component you scored as a 3, and run through the same 1-10 scorecard exercise for the second-tier elements.

This time, you might score these components as 1, 3, 3, 5, 8 and 2. There's clearly a lot of work to do in this area and the scorecard exercise has just helped you decide in which order to tackle it.

The first process to benefit from your attention (working together with your department head or the person who will execute the process – remember, this isn't to be dictated from above) is the main flywheel component that scored lowest and then the lowest-scoring component on that second-tier flywheel.

An important note at this point: what do you think the chances are of turning a 1 into a 10? Realistically, that's unlikely to happen, at least in the first iteration of this process.

I quite like the rule of two: aiming to improve your 1-10 score on each process by just two points. Turning a 1 into a 10 is an impossible task, while turning a 1 into a 3 is achievable for most. A 3 to a 5? Yep, we could do that. And 7 to a 9? It won't be easy, but we're already pretty good at this task, so we just need to raise the bar a little higher.

In our example, we turn the 1 to a 3, the 2 to a 4, the two 3s to 5s, and the 5 to a 7. I'd probably leave the 8 alone, considering that good enough for now. There's far greater low hanging fruit improvements to be had elsewhere. Suddenly, that 3 on the main flywheel is now a 5. It's still the worst part of our business, but no longer significantly worse and we can always revisit the processes *after* we've ensured these are adhered to consistently, with a view to taking that 5 to a 7.

When I ran through this exercise a few years ago, I identified Retention First as the weakest point of my flywheel. I was a marketer at heart and naturally leaned into my ability to win new business. My frustrations grew, however, as customers I worked hard to win then left just a few months later. I felt like I was having to work harder and harder, filling a leaky bucket, and I blamed my team for not doing *their* job of keeping customers happy.

Well, after a few years of blaming everyone else (and nothing changing), I decided to actually do something about it myself. Having scored a measly 4/10 for Retention First on my main flywheel, I opened up my second-tier Retention First flywheel and gave myself the following scores:

- Reinforce the core belief – 1/10.
- Weave into the community – 2/10.
- Signpost the pathway – 2/10.
- Encourage two-way communication – 2/10.
- Deliver on our promises – 8/10.
- Encourage personal development – 8/10.

A few parts of my retention strategy were working well (delivering on our promises and encouraging long-standing members to keep working on their own personal development). However, all this good work was undone on the next trip around, with all momentum lost and my Retention First flywheel almost grinding to a halt thanks to our failure to reinforce the core belief.

Those 8s don't make much difference after a 1 and three 2s! It was clear where my attention was needed. Again, I didn't aim for perfection. Leaving the 8s alone, I looked to increase the lower scores by the rule of two, taking the 1 to a 3 and the three 2s to 4s.

I needed to better reinforce our core belief: that leaving your business 1% better each week is the key to steady, predictable, sustainable growth over the long term, thanks to the exponential power of compounding. This is a belief that I personally live and breathe and to which I credit all of my success. The problem was, I kept pretty quiet about my belief. I'd mention it every now and then, but not consistently.

So I introduced a new process – a weekly "Monday Morning Motivation" video sent to all members with an inspirational message centred around this core belief of weekly 1% improvement. I created a mock road sign for "One Percent Way", which sits on my desk in all of our coaching calls, podcasts, masterclasses, and serves as a constant reminder – to myself, my team and to members – that we are *all* on the One Percent Way, because we *all* share the same core belief of improving our businesses (and ourselves) by 1% each week.

A simple weekly video and a visual reminder elevated "Reinforce the core belief" from a 1/10 to 3/10. It was no longer the worst performing component on my Retention First flywheel.

Next, I looked at how we integrate new members into the community. This was a pretty poor 2/10. The existing community was thriving, but there wasn't really a strategic plan to weave new One Percenters into the group. To rectify this, I created a new "Meet the Members" coaching call, which takes place during our March and September intakes. This call has no educational benefit and is purely a social event to allow new members to meet existing ones and get to know them. Boom! Weaving new members into the community crept up to 4/10 as a result.

I improved our signposting of relevant content by rewriting our welcome emails to show new members how they'll get the most out of the club, adding clear directions to the most relevant content for them and explaining what happens, where and when. Another few days of work and another 2/10 turned into a 4/10.

I added plenty of leading questions into the welcome emails to encourage members to reply and included new pure outreach messages, which improved "Encourage two-way communication" by a point or two.

After a few weeks' work, the new scores on the doors were:

- Reinforce the core belief – 3/10.
- Weave into the community – 4/10.
- Signpost the pathway – 4/10.
- Encourage two-way communication – 4/10.
- Deliver on our promises – 8/10.
- Encourage personal development – 8/10.

At this point, I would have given the Retention First component of the main flywheel a rating of 4/10 – a two-point improvement, but still the weakest point of our primary flywheel.

However, once I was satisfied that these new processes were sustained consistently, I went back to work, identifying even more processes that could be added or improved (as well as some that needed removing altogether as they were causing friction).

My process was the same: go around the flywheel, scanning for the weakest points. Work with my team to identify improvements that will likely boost the scores. Implement small improvements, one at a time and ensure that they are executed consistently, rather than perfectly. Then, go around the flywheel again. And again. And again.

The thread of 1% improvement runs throughout our entire flywheel now. Our "welcome" sequence for new members currently stands at a whopping 285 emails, delivered over a period of more than five years. It's grown so big that we've even given it a name – the One Percent Way. Every email in the One Percent Way helps achieve at least one element from the Retention First flywheel – to reinforce the core belief, forge a stronger community, signpost our best content, encourage two-way communication, deliver on our promises, and help members stay on the path of constant, never-ending improvement – not only of their business, but of themselves.

We overhauled the members' website – creating new content to reinforce the core belief, make connecting with the community easier, vastly improved signposting to our best content, and encouraging real-life feedback from members.

Treating One Percenters to the prawn sandwich experience at Plymouth Argyle enables us to spend an afternoon reinforcing the core belief (explaining how Argyle are currently benefiting from years of stacking up 1% improvements in every aspect of the club – from scouting and data analysis to corporate hospitality and superstore sales). It also helps us cement each member's place in the community – making connections and introductions to other members as we get to know them better. It involves several hours of two-way communication, helping us discover how to best help them achieve their goals.

If you recall, I even wrote an entire book that is only available to One Percenters. Over the course of 100 pages or so, I explain to new members how powerful this core belief of leaving your business 1% better each week really is. I introduce around a dozen long-standing One Percenters, who share their stories and explain how they get the most from their membership. This helps new members feel as if they know the OGs, signposts the pathway for new members to follow and helps us deliver on our promises.

I even use the book to encourage two-way communication (as well as fanning the flames of the core belief once more) with my closing words on the final page:

> *"I look forward to seeing your results – email me john@bigidea.co.uk to let me know what 1% wins you've been stacking up – and what impact that's having on your ambitious, lifestyle business. After all, I may need to send you a four-foot-high inflatable pink flamingo!"*

Ah, yes! The flamingo. As mentioned earlier, the pink bird came to represent everything the One Percent Club stands for. This status symbol helps me reinforce the core belief without uttering a word. All I need to do is ensure members associate the flamingo with the core belief. Once this is explained (via a video in the members' area, the welcome email sequence, in the One Percent Way book, and on the "Getting to Know You" call), the flamingo subtly reminds members with each appearance.

That's why there's a flamboyance of flamingos throughout our business: on the front cover of The One Percent Way book, in the footer of the members' area, a neon-pink flamingo light illuminated in every video, and all manner of flamingo paraphernalia deployed at every opportunity. I'm now the "proud" owner of several pieces of flamingo-print clothing, as well as my very own 4ft high inflatable. Hardly a day goes by without a One Percenter sharing a photo with the group of a flamingo they've seen somewhere on their travels.

So, what's the end result of 18 months of constant, never-ending improvement of our weakest component? You can flick back a few pages to check out the starting scores but here is how I would judge our Retention First flywheel today:

- Reinforce the core belief – 9/10.
- Weave into the community – 7/10.

- Signpost the pathway – 7/10.
- Encourage two-way communication – 7/10.
- Deliver on our promises – 9/10.
- Encourage personal development – 9/10.

There's still work to be done, but we've more than doubled our average score from less than 4/10 to a healthy 8/10. Crucially, those 1s and 2s are no longer killing our momentum.

I can see results in member retention as well, with the average lifetime of a member doubling in the past 18 months. What began as a "leaky bucket" – the weakest point of our business – has become one of our strongest. But not without a lot of work, a steadfast dedication to improving the process bit by bit (1% each week), and complete buy-in from the whole team.

NOTHING MEASURED, NOTHING MANAGED

I've made it clear that delegation, not abdication, is key to a successful False EXIT. Yet, when it comes to your finances, I'd actually advise you to do *neither*. The numbers are your job. You must obsess over them, know them inside-out, and watch them like a hawk. Delegate almost any bucket-carrying task you like, but please, for the sake of your sanity, do not delegate the numbers. The numbers are the most important thing for a False EXIT-ed business owner to monitor.

Each morning, I sit with my coffee poring over data from dozens of sources via a Minority Report-style, 24/7 live reporting dashboard, which gives me access to all the data I need.

At a glance, I know how many leads the team generated compared to last month. I can see how many of those leads converted to sales, as well as which products are selling (and which are not). I know for sure whether our SEO rankings are improving (and if so, which ones). I can view cashflow forecasts, revenue trends, and website performance. I can benchmark conversion percentages, lifetime values, churn rates and about 100 other metrics. Via this dashboard, I can monitor the numbers that dictate the health of my business. You *must* keep an eye on the metrics that matter in your business. If you don't, they will suffer. Once again, you should not delegate the numbers to anyone else and certainly never abdicate them.

Before I invested in an automated dashboard, I manually compiled a KPI (key performance indicator) report each month. I would diligently pull off reports, download data, and export the company's results for a wide range of measurables. I'd document our largest transactions, evaluate the performance of our products, and calculate our most lucrative partnerships. I'd monitor the performance of our marketing, tracking sales all the way back to their original source to ensure our most profitable sources were fully exploited, while less profitable ones were ignored or improved.

At a glance, I could see whether our customer base was growing or shrinking, whether paid members were staying for longer or disappearing sooner. I could see who owed us money, how late they paid, as well as who we owed money to – and how much of the money in our bank was actually *our* money. Because I knew my numbers, I knew exactly how many leads were coming into the business, where those leads were coming from, and how much we were paying for them. I knew which email had the greatest impact in terms of open rates, click-throughs, and conversions, helping shape our future marketing strategy.

I could see the impact of our SEO work, when our bounce rate (the percentage of visitors who almost immediately leave the website – a good indicator that they *didn't* find what they were looking for), number of pageviews and time spent on site all improved.

I could compare the current month's data against recent and historic trends. Tracking three and 12-month averages, I know what's "normal" and can investigate any deviation from that.

Finally, I asked each team member to write a few paragraphs explaining what happened in their department last month. This added some context to the raw data and often served as an early warning system that a problem was imminent, but not yet reflected in the data – or that an anomaly in the metrics had been spotted, investigated and dealt with.

This monthly KPI report used to take me around half a day to collate and another half-day to review. The ROI was off the charts. Every month without fail, I would discover *something*. An early warning of an imminent problem we could nip in the bud. An opportunity to be exploited. An area of the business which was working particularly well or particularly badly. There was always some low-hanging fruit to be found in the numbers.

And then I started writing my first book.

Having massively underestimated the work involved, the *Big Ideas... for Small Businesses* project took over my life for the best part of a year. I essentially took a False EXIT (without knowing what I know now – and what I'm preaching in this book) and removed myself from the day-to-day operations of the business. And because I no longer had time to collate and review the KPI reports, the numbers were not looked at for several months.

Eventually, during a break in writing, I trawled through a few months of missed metrics and what I found shocked me. I discovered simple tap-in opportunities not taken. Tiny problems were ignored and had grown into large problems, which were also ignored. Almost every metric I looked at had deteriorated in the month's I'd been AWOL.

And that was the problem: I was absent without leave. It wasn't even a case of abdicating, not delegating, because – as I said at the start of this section – the numbers are not a thing you should either abdicate from or delegate. They say "what gets measured, gets managed". Well, for several months, while I was bashing away at my keyboard, nothing was getting measured and nothing was getting managed.

I don't regret taking the time away from my business to write the book, but without a doubt, my abdication from measuring what matters had a significant cost that I hadn't anticipated.

That's why I now have an automated dashboard at my fingertips 24/7, containing real-time data (as well as historical trends) on the metrics that matter most. Working with my team, it took several days of work, over many months, to get the dashboard working exactly as I wanted it. But once it was up and running, we never needed to manually collate another KPI report again – saving half a day's work each month.

I still need to review the data regularly, though. Low hanging fruit is only valuable if someone's there to harvest it before it falls to the ground and rots. The ability to nip problems in the bud is only valuable if those problems actually *get* nipped before they grow.

When you take a False EXIT, there will be a few tasks that you simply cannot delegate and certainly shouldn't abdicate. Reviewing your company's metrics is definitely one of these.

If you were a specialist consultant in a hospital, you wouldn't personally measure the each patient's vital signs yourself on an hourly basis. But you would expect someone to collect that data and make it available for you to review on your daily rounds. It's the nurse's job to collect and store the data, to measure what matters. Your job is to *manage* what's been measured, to spot the early warning signs of danger lurking in the future, the green shoots of recovery or the low-hanging fruit of an opportunity.

TRUST, YET VERIFY

Monitoring a patient's heart rate at regular intervals gives doctors useful data to chart recovery. But having the machine set off a "red flag" alarm should the patient flatline saves lives.

What red flag systems do you have in your business? Are you alerted before your sales flatline or before the bank account runs dry? Can you trust that what should be happening, is happening? Do you trust your staff to do as you've asked, yet verify that they *are*? Can you trust they won't steal from you, but verify that they aren't? If you trust your clients to pay on time, you should also verify that they *do*.

Red flag systems enable you to trust, but verify.

Once you know the historical "norm" for your metrics, consider which measurements matter most and then set up red flag alerts should these mission-critical metrics deviate. I have red flag systems to alert me if customers fail to pay their bills on time, our SEO rankings change significantly or if our cashflow drops below a certain level.

I trust my clients to pay on time, but verify that they do. I trust the marketing systems I've created will continue to work, yet I verify that they are.

I trust my team, but I verify that my trust in them is justified.

Our team meetings used to be a 60-minute natter about how things are going, what everyone's been up to, with constant deviations into areas that have no impact on the business whatsoever. These were all-hands meetings, so the combined cost to the business in salaries alone for that hour was several hundred pounds. The ROI on that? To the nearest whole number, zero.

So, we turned our weekly team meeting into a weekly metrics meeting. Instead of being an hour-long gossip-fest, we made metrics the star of the show. Another automated dashboard was built, with real-time data on our three most important metrics for this quarter. These metrics could be focusing on increasing sales, reducing churn, improving the quality of a product or optimising a marketing channel.

Each week, our progress towards these three metrics is measured and discussed. If we're not on track to hit the metrics target, we discuss how to get back on track and what each individual can do to help. Additionally, each team member has their own individual metrics, again, usually three. Marketing may have targets for leads captured, sales made and revenue generated, while Customer Service's numbers may focus on email response time, increased retention rates and growing the lifetime value of each member.

If you've got multiple people working in the same department, you have the added bonus of benchmarking individual performance. You may think you've got an A-grade player bringing in four sales a week until you start benchmarking and realise that someone else does six a week – and that your supposed superstar is actually coasting.

This doesn't need to be high tech or super complicated either. Henry Ford once painted a large "6" on the factory floor. When the workers arrived in the morning, Ford explained: "That's the number of cars the night crew built." By the time the overnight shift returned, the day crew had painted a "7" on the floor. From that moment, both crews were aware of the other team's performance – and both raised their game.

One Percenter John O'Sullivan felt one of his team wasn't pulling their weight compared to the others, so he took a leaf out of Henry Ford's book and put up a whiteboard on the office wall, showing the previous day's sales (as well as month-to-date totals) for each person. John saw an almost immediate impact. With his sub-par performance now glaringly obvious for all to see, the "freeloader" suddenly began to use his time more productively, closing sales rather than chatting about the big match or last night's TV.

There's no room for freeloaders, passengers or moochers in a small business. Benchmarking roots them out. Trust people to perform, yet verify that they do.

It's important for team members to own their metrics. They should feel their metrics are something they can control and understand how their numbers contribute towards the overall company metrics. Any discussion about "what I've been doing this week" should always come back to the numbers, either confirming you're on course to hit your metrics or working out how to get back on track.

Keeping conversations focused on metrics does two things:

1. They remind everyone what really matters. We're not here to focus on busy work. Instead, we're aiming for this specific goal. And we can all help to achieve that goal by hitting our metrics.
2. They ensure there's no place to hide. Yes, we trust you to do a good job – but we also verify. Time and again the pattern repeats: the right people want to be measured. They want their metrics publicly displayed for all to see – because, like the Ford workers replacing that "6" with a "7", they're immensely proud of them. If someone shies away from being measured, that's a huge red flag and an indication they possibly shouldn't be on your bus.

What red flag systems could you put in place? Could you employ mystery shoppers, add yourself (under a different name) to your CRM or set little "tests" to ensure quality control? Why not visit the front lines unannounced and do a few spot checks or a full-blown audit? Whatever it takes to verify your trust.

And trust, you must. If you don't trust your team, you will create overly complicated systems and processes to insure against that distrust. When you don't trust someone to deliver, you constantly micro-manage them, reminding them of deadlines, triple-checking their work – or worse, end up doing their job yourself, telling yourself that it's the only way to get the work done right. That can only lead to more bucket-carrying misery.

The right people, armed with the right vision and values, the right decision-making framework and the right systems should be worthy of your trust. A simple red flag system enables you to trust, yet verify.

HOW LONG IS A PIECE OF SYSTEMISATION?

How long do you think it will take to capture all of your systems, organise them and actually use them? Whatever answer you've just come up with, double it. Then, double it again. And again.

Most people drastically underestimate how long it will take to fully systemise their business, often by a magnitude of months or even years. I've yet to meet a business owner who got it right the first time. Most don't get it nailed on the second, third or fourth attempts either. Systemising my business was my No1 priority for the best part of 18 months – and it's still a work in progress.

Systemisation isn't a one-time project. Rather than aiming for a one-and-done solution (which will probably be obsolete in a few years anyway), adopt a systems mindset and spend the rest of your days constantly improving each system you encounter.

Systems will form the bulk of the pipeline that will absolve you of your bucket-carrying duties. This creates a new role for you – chief pipeline officer, responsible for improving the efficiency and effectiveness, maintaining key areas, and replacing worn parts. Less firefighting, more fire prevention. After all, now that you're not carrying those buckets any more, what are you actually going to do with all this time on your hands?

8. LET IT GO! LET IT GO!

> *"I don't want to be the CEO of anything. I rather hate it and I would much prefer to spend my time on design and engineering,"*
>
> – *Elon Musk*

So now you've learned the False EXIT framework in a nutshell. Class dismissed! Off you go, out into the real world, ready to put the theory into practice and exit the day-to-day running of your business. See ya! Bye.

What's that? You've got questions? Of course you do. And in this section, I'll answer the most common questions that I receive when helping business owners to put down their buckets and start building their pipeline.

If you read all this and still feel like your specific concern or query hasn't been answered, please email me at john@bigidea.co.uk and I'll help you connect the dots.

MY BUSINESS RELIES ON ME. IT *NEEDS* ME. HOW COULD I EVER EXIT?

I'll answer that question with one of my own: why does your business rely on you? Is it because of complexity? The more complex your business, the more "only you" can run it. Perhaps, as I described the process of capturing your flywheel – those five or six key principles which run your entire operation – you found yourself yelling at the book "but my business is more complicated than that".

Well, if so, then I would remind you that Amazon – a trillion dollar company, with more than a million employees, and hundreds of millions of both customers and products – runs on just five key principles. You can always simplify and if you're going to take a False EXIT, you *must* simplify. Complexity is the enemy – one that will prevent you from ever exiting.

If complexity isn't the issue, then perhaps we need to look closer to home. Is it possible that you *want* your business to rely on you, because it makes you feel important, significant or essential? No one likes to feel they're replaceable. Many small business owners like to justify their existence, telling themselves their business wouldn't survive (let alone thrive) without them. As a result, they dream up busy work and then complain they're always busy.

These guys aren't the Chief Fire Prevention Officer in their company. No, they're pyromaniacs – lighting fires so they can be the hero who extinguishes them. It's self-sabotage of the highest degree. Easy to recognise in others, less so in yourself. That's why I'm being brutal. No one is truly indispensable. Remember, Microsoft multiplied in value by 14 times after Bill Gates left. Apple 7x'd their share price after Steve Jobs died.

"But customers demand me." If this is true, then it's a monster of your own making. Customers want you because they've always had you. You've done a great job for them in the past, so they trust you to do so again. Or perhaps you've put yourself front and centre in your marketing, so people think you *are* the business.

If this is the case, you need to wean clients off you, adjusting your marketing to include the whole team. Start by insisting all new clients are looked after by your team – not you. Then, you can give existing clients a choice. They can either receive the same standard of service from one of your team for the same price they currently pay – or they can choose to pay 30 to 50% more for you to do the same work. Eventually, I'd be keen to edge this premium pricing higher and higher as you edge further towards your False EXIT, eventually charging at least twice as much for access to you.

Given the choice of paying a large premium, many who "only want you" will suddenly change their tune and give your team a chance. Sure, some will still want you and be willing to pay the premium. But others will soon realise your team is just as good as you – if not better!

But what if your team *isn't* as good as you? Well, that's an area to address as you transition to working *on* the business, ensuring you've got the right people on the bus, the wrong people off the bus, and the right people in the right seats. It's a crucial part of the pipeline for you to improve through training, coaching, and mentoring to ensure your team has access to the systems and processes they need to reach the same level of competency that clients have come to expect from you.

I'VE HEARD HORROR STORIES OF STAFF STEALING CLIENTS AND SETTING UP ON THEIR OWN. HOW DO I PREVENT MY TEAM FROM STEALING MY BUSINESS?

I read about a couple who emigrated to Australia, leaving their team running their financial services business in the UK. Twelve months later, they popped back to Blighty, only to discover that they'd been locked out of everything – the bank account, CRM, emails, website. The team had even changed the locks on the front door of the office. They were literally locked out of their business, which their team had stolen from under their noses.

What a nightmare! And I'm sure it was horrible for the business owners involved. But let's be objective here for a moment. Why are horror stories so memorable? Because they're incredibly catastrophic – but also incredibly rare. When a crazed axe murderer goes on a killing spree, taking three lives, it's headline news nationwide. But around 189,000 people die every single day and, other than those directly affected, no one blinks an eye.

So yes, your team might steal from you. They could dip their hand in the till, pinch your client list and set up in competition with you, or – as in the extreme case above – steal your entire business and lock you out. But it's extremely rare and there is plenty you can do to reduce the risk of it happening to you.

First and foremost, the *right people* are far less likely to steal from you. If your team consists of the right people, who truly share your vision and values, stealing probably isn't going to be in their nature. That's not to say they would *never* steal – but it isn't going to come naturally to them. There typically needs to be a trigger to prompt them to override their usual values.

This is why it's so important not to hire dickheads or tolerate bad apples. Overlooking someone who clashes with your vision and values because they're good at their job might work if you're there to keep an eye on them, reining them in when they start colouring outside of the lines. But leaving them to their own devices is a recipe for disaster.

Of course, even the shiniest, tastiest apple has the potential to go bad if left and this is why I've encouraged – nay, demanded – that you set up "trust, yet verify" red flag systems to spot small problems before they become big ones. I would hazard a guess that the expats who found themselves locked out of their business didn't have red flag systems. They trusted, without verifying. They abdicated (and emigrated) rather than delegated.

Trust yet verify alerts work to prevent theft and wrongdoing in two ways:

1. They catch thieves and scoundrels early. Red flag systems are like a smoke detector – they alert you to the early warning signs before they become a major issue.
2. They're a deterrent in themselves. If people know they're being monitored – if they know that you not only trust but also verify – they're more likely to *be* trustworthy.

In a Halloween experiment by social scientist Arthur Beaman, child trick or treaters were directed to a bowl of sweets on a table and told to take one sweet each. The researchers then excused themselves, leaving the kids alone with the candy. You can probably guess what happened – a third of the children (33.7%) took more than one sweet.

But when the researchers added a mirror above the bowl (so the children could see themselves taking the sweets), the theft rate dropped by almost three quarters to just 8.9%. In a similar study, adding a photo of a pair of eyes above a "honesty box" led to a 150% increase in payments. Trust, yet verify.

You'll never be able to fully reduce the risk of business theft to zero, but you can greatly minimise it – by hiring the right people, creating a culture around shared vision and values, giving your team frameworks to help make decisions with ease, and systems to help them do the best work of their lives.

Most "business thieves" feel that the business owner doesn't care, wouldn't notice, and doesn't share their vision. They feel they can do better, creating a little world of their own. There may be resentment, where they feel they're doing all the work while you reap all the rewards (I've had team members in the past who thought that every penny we collected in turnover went straight to my pocket).

But, if you communicate the reality, compensate them fairly for the contribution they make, and demonstrate that you trust them (but *verify* that trust is warranted), it slashes the risk of a horror story.

I DON'T HAVE THE TIME TO IMPLEMENT ALL OF THIS. WILL I EVER BE ABLE TO EXIT?

Ah, the age old "too busy" business owner conundrum. You're too busy working *in* the business to work *on* the business and you're busy *in* the business because you haven't spent enough time working *on* the business. I'm afraid there is only one way out of this vicious circle and that's to carve out the time to work on your pipeline, rather than carrying buckets. To work on the pipeline, rather than carrying buckets.

Remember our bucket-carrying brothers Barry and Paul? When Paul decided to build a pipeline to transport the water down the hill to the village, he didn't have the time either. He spent all day carrying buckets of water and then used evenings and weekends – the time he previously used for rest – to start on his pipeline. And that pipeline wasn't built overnight, either. It took an investment of time and effort upfront, in order to save time and effort later.

Again, Paul didn't *find* the time to build his pipeline. No, he *made* the time. He blocked that time out and worked exclusively *on* his pipeline rather than *in* his bucket-carrying business, even though, in the short term, it meant longer hours for less money.

He kept going until, one day, with his pipeline complete, he needed never to carry a bucket again – while brother Barry was still moaning that he couldn't find the time.

The demands of your business aren't going to meekly step aside while you plan your False EXIT. No, you're going to have to do what Paul did and choose which buckets you will continue to carry for the time being – even if that means working longer hours for less money – and which buckets you will no longer lift yourself. Over time, just as Paul did, you can make elements of your pipeline operational, allowing more of your bucket-carrying time to be reallocated towards pipeline construction.

Atomic Habits author James Clear says: "Rome wasn't built in a day, but they were laying bricks every hour. You don't have to build everything you want today, just lay a brick."

It might take you six months or six years but one thing is undeniably true: if you don't start today and continue tomorrow, you'll *never* exit.

I'VE TRIED LETTING GO BEFORE AND EVERY TIME I HAVE, IT'S GONE HORRIBLY WRONG. WILL I EVER REALLY BE ABLE TO TRUST SOMEONE ELSE WITH MY BUSINESS?

Letting go of your "baby" is scary. It feels like an unmanned car about to swerve into a ditch until you grab the steering wheel at the last minute. The danger is that, like the "too busy working *in* the business to work *on* the business" dilemma, this can become a self-fulfilling prophecy. You don't trust your team, so you snatch that steering wheel back, guiding the business back to safety.

But, because you always grab the wheel, your team never learns to drive the car. Circus performers will tell you that the best way to learn to walk a tightrope is without a safety net. You'll never develop the twitch muscle memory required to truly master the skill if the safety net always breaks your fall.

It's the same with your team. They need to know you *truly* trust them with your business. In order to develop their own muscle memory, they need to be allowed to fail, to make mistakes. Show me a tightrope-walker who's never broken a bone and I'll show you one who's never ventured more than a foot off the ground.

When you let your team take control, it won't be perfect the first time. Or the second. Or the third, or even the 27th time you let go. But it will get better each time as you course correct; adjusting the decision-making frameworks, coaching your team on your vision and values, ensuring you've truly got the right people (in the right seats), and helping them to design the systems they need to do their best work.

Your team is not you. They're not clones of you or robots sent out to perform exactly as you would. Each is their own person with their own unique skill set and they will think and behave slightly differently to you. Have you ever sat in the passenger seat of a car and tried stomping the brake pedal (that isn't there) because the person driving tends to brake a little later than you? If so, (and you're still here to tell the tale), then everything worked out, didn't it? You gave control of the car to the other person. They drove it slightly differently to you. Given half a chance, you would have slammed on the brakes and grabbed the steering wheel – but you didn't. And it was fine.

Letting go takes a lot of getting used to especially if (like me) you're used to being a control freak. Sometimes you need to sit on your hands, keep your mouth shut and let your team decide, let them fail, let them course correct. If they're the right people, in the right seats, with a shared vision, they'll be motivated to achieve that vision – and more than capable of doing so.

Let go of the small stuff first. Let go for an hour or an afternoon. Build from there. Raise that tightrope half an inch each week.

Remember, trust works both ways. Of course, you need to be able to trust your team with your business. But they also need to be able to trust you to leave them alone and let them do their best work. They need to know that you trust them and won't grab the steering wheel at the first sign of an oncoming car, a narrow lane or a bend in the road.

IT SEEMS LIKE A LOT OF EXTRA WORK. WHY DON'T I JUST SELL?

To fully maximise your sale price, you'll likely have to do much of this work anyway. One of the first questions any potential purchaser of your business is likely to ask is: "How reliant is this business on you?" If your answer is anything other than, "I'm not involved in the day-to-day operations whatsoever", the price you're likely to attract will diminish significantly.

I would estimate each working day you are required to work in your business each week reduces your multiple (the number of years profit a business sells for) by the same amount.

Don't believe that investors would pay five times more for a business that doesn't require the business owner to operate it, versus one that requires him or her full time? Do some research. Look at recent business sales in your sector. Evaluate the multiples and how involved the outgoing owners were. Speak to business brokers who buy and sell businesses all day long and they'll tell you there's a huge correlation there.

The more your business needs you to run it, the less it's worth. The less it needs you, the more it's worth. Simple.

You may decide, after implementing the False EXIT framework, that you've actually created a very sellable business and want to cash in. Well, that's the beauty of a False EXIT: putting these frameworks in place could enable you to make a very *real* exit and for more money that you'd have otherwise received.

Of course, if you want to keep the golden goose, you'll be in a perfect place to enjoy your False EXIT. After exiting the day-to-day operations, your actual hourly rate – the amount of money you actually withdrew from your business last year, divided by the number of hours you actually worked (there's a calculator for working this out in the resources) – should be embarrassingly high. You may even find you start to receive unsolicited enquiries from people wanting to buy your business. That certainly never happened when I was working 100-plus hours a week carrying my own buckets!

HOW CAN I EXIT? MY TEAM JUST DOESN'T CARE!

Do you have the right people? Are they in the right seats? Do they share your vision and values? Do they really not care? Or have you simply not allowed them to care by snatching the steering wheel from them one too many times?

Captain D. Michael Abrashoff transformed the USS Benfold from the "worst ship in the Navy" into one of the best. When Abrashoff assumed command of the guided missile destroyer, he described a "dysfunctional ship" with "a sullen crew that resented being there and could not wait to get out of the Navy". Yet, within three years, Abrashoff had turned the Benfold into the highest-performing ship in its class without changing a single member of his crew. Nobody got off the bus. Instead, they were handed the keys to drive it.

"The more responsibility I gave up," Captain Abrashoff explains in his 2002 book *It's Your Ship*, "the more command I got. In the beginning, people kept asking my permission to do things. Eventually, I told the crew: 'It's your ship. You're responsible for it. Make a decision and see what happens.'"

Benfold's sailors were used to being told what to do, as well as when and how to do it and then usually berated for getting it wrong before senior officers grabbed the steering wheel at the last minute. Abrashoff's predecessors all warned him: "These guys don't care." Undeterred, he decided to see what happened when his sailors were actually given the opportunity to care.

It took a while for the "it's your ship" mantra to sink in – for the sailors to realise this wasn't yet another management gimmick, but a genuine demonstration of their commander's trust in their ability. And, over time, the culture shifted from one where no one cares to one where everyone cares.

Show me an organisation in which employees take true ownership and I will show you one that beats its competitors. Of course, this transition wasn't plain sailing (literally) all the way and Captain Abrashoff had to course correct often. Although he had the right people on his bus, they still needed to know how and where to drive it. And that meant trusting them, rather than blaming them as he grabbed the steering wheel.

Abrashoff explains: "Whenever I could not get the results I wanted, I swallowed my temper and turned inward to see if I was part of the problem. I asked myself three questions: 1) Did I clearly articulate the goals? 2) Did I give people enough time and resources to accomplish the task? 3) Did I give them enough training? I discovered that 90% of the time, I was at least as much a part of the problem as my people were."

If you genuinely feel your team doesn't care, you must consider, as Captain Abrashoff did, that you could be as much a part of the problem as they are. Have you clearly articulated the company's goals, especially the vision and values? Have you given your team enough time and resources to accomplish the task? Have you given them enough training? And would they give the same answers if I asked them?

Crucially, do they consider it to be their bus or yours? This sense of ownership is what turned USS Benfold into "the best damn ship in the

Navy" and it could turn your business into the best damn company in your sector.

WHAT'S THE POINT? I JUST CAN'T FACE IT ANYMORE. I HATE MY BUSINESS AND I JUST WANT SHOT OF IT!

We've all been there, believe me – casting envious glances at the people who leave their desks at 5pm and who don't even think about work until 9am the following day. The simple life without sleepless nights worrying about meeting payroll, losing a key client or the constant fear that everything will come crashing down around you. I've been running small businesses for more than two decades and even I still have these moments of self-doubt. Twenty-plus years and I still think I'm going to be found out at any moment and unmasked as the pretender I was when I first picked up a copy of *Internet Marketing for Dummies* in 2000.

It's perfectly normal for small business owners to hate their creation at times – especially after years of constant bucket-carrying and complete reliance on you. But consider this: do you really hate your business or do you just hate what it's become?

If you could remove yourself from the daily grind and elevate yourself to the position of shareholder, with a board of directors below you running the business (almost) exactly the way you want, would you still hate it?

It's pointless spending a few years building a pipeline for a business you'd still hate. But, if it's simply the day-to-day stress and overwhelm that's causing you pain, then a False EXIT could relieve your torment.

Figuring out what's causing your suffering requires thinking time. Block out an hour or so and go somewhere quiet where you won't be disturbed. Grab a blank piece of paper and write down how your business makes you *feel*. Without wanting to put words in your mouth, here's some common complaints:

- Stressed.
- Overwhelmed.
- Worthless.
- Busy fool.
- I'm the only one who cares.

Next, write down everything you do for your business – everything from your flywheels that currently require you. Then, connect the two lists. Draw a line from what you do to how it makes you feel. For example, "Being on call at weekends" would have a line linking it to making me feel "On edge all the time". Meanwhile, "Getting results for clients" has a direct line to me feeling "Proud".

Once this is complete, you should start to see the root causes of your discomfort and can begin to tackle them.

I performed this exercise after my "I can't do this anymore!" moment, snapping at Jason in my kitchen all those years ago. I wrote down everything that I did on a daily, weekly and monthly basis, as well as all my high-level responsibilities, and then drew connections between what I "had" to do and how those responsibilities made me feel.

On one sheet of paper, I listed my feelings about my businesses. I felt stressed and overwhelmed, as if I was constantly chasing my tail, trying to keep all the plates spinning, worrying they would all come crashing to the ground the minute I took my eye off them.

And on the other five(!) sheets were all the tasks I was solely responsible for: multiple businesses, high-stakes investments, time-sensitive demands, and the livelihoods of everyone on my team. I didn't hate my business; I hated what it had become. It was a monster of my own creation.

The remedy to my self-torture was to drop most of the buckets I was carrying. I shut down entire businesses, liquidated investments, simplified processes and removed myself as the godlike genius responsible for the successful spinning of every plate in every business. Your prescription could be different and it may even involve a full exit rather than a false one. Getting out of your business altogether might be more important to you than getting out of the day-to-day.

Either way, it's an exercise that's very revealing and can be incredibly rewarding.

WHAT WILL I ACTUALLY DO AFTER I'VE EXITED?

What's your plan post-exit? Work on your golf handicap? Sip mojitos poolside? Take up a new hobby? And what about the second week? Or the second month – or year? What's going to get you out of bed in the morning, let alone fulfil you long term? A lack of purpose can be fatal. Literally.

A study of retirees at oil company Shell discovered that those who took early retirement aged 55 were 89% more likely to die in their first ten years after retirement compared to those who took their pension at 65. So much for having extra golden years to enjoy life!

It's time to abandon the old, 40/40/40 plan – where you spend 40 years working 40 hours a week to then retire on 40% of your income. Why can't we bring some of that spare time forward from retirement to enjoy now while we still have our health? In return, let's extend our sense of usefulness, fulfilment and purpose into our latter years.

Since my own False EXIT, I've home-schooled my children, spent time with my elderly parents, prioritised my health (mental and physical), travelled the world and written four books for ambitious, lifestyle business owners. I'd love to tell you I've improved my golf handicap too, but that would be a lie!

I've also continued to give tremendous value to my business. Remember, a False EXIT is about delegation, not abdication. It's enabled me to "nip out" of my business for a few weeks or a few months and then return, devoting my time to the continued, never-ending improvement of the pipeline (now that my bucket-carrying skills are no longer required).

When I was carrying those buckets myself, I used to spend around four hours per day answering customer enquiries. When I first outsourced this, I wondered what on Earth I would do with all this new-found time on my hands. I'd just gained an extra 20 hours per week. Would I be bored out of my brain or sit around, twiddling my thumbs all day?

Of course, three weeks later, I'd filled those 20 hours and was working flat out again – this time on improving the customer service pipeline. Optimising my business, rather than optimising my own busy-ness. I give the greatest value to my business, not by being the best bucket carrier in the company, but by creating evergreen assets – improving the pipeline, making any uplifts in the company's performance permanent.

Nowadays, I still work hard for my business – not carrying buckets because I have to, but improving the pipeline because I want to. I get to coach my team, rather than micro-manage them. The more I mould my team in my own vision and values, the better the pipeline works. It's taken a little trial and error, but I feel I now have the right people, armed with my decision-making framework, carrying the buckets for me. They're people I can trust, following systems they can trust.

Occasionally, I need to verify that trust is warranted. And sometimes, it isn't. I'm not going to tell you that everything will be sunshine and rainbows from here on – this isn't a Disney movie. But it is a lot better than the alternative: spending the rest of your days carrying buckets until you physically (or mentally) can't lift another bucket.

So how do I spend my days now? How do I continue to give value to the business that – let's not forget – I still own? I spend a few hours each week coaching the team – soft on tactics, hard on strategy – helping them to improve and make better decisions without me.

I can give tremendous value to the company by creating evergreen assets, improving the pipeline permanently using the principles of constant, never-ending improvement. Crucially though, the business is not dependent on me day-to-day, which means I can "nip out" for a fortnight's holiday (leaving the laptop at home), an entire quarter working on another business or the best part of a year writing a book.

Because I have my "trust, yet verify" systems in place, I can keep an eye on the metrics, monitor any red flags, perform fire prevention work, and ensure the team is on track. The business doesn't suffer from my absence – it actually benefits from it. I work best in a HIIT style. For the uninitiated, HIIT stands for High Intensity Interval Training. It's a form of physical workout that is incredibly demanding, yet devastatingly effective. As the name suggests, you work at a high intensity – giving it absolutely everything you've got, but only for a short period of time – usually 20 to 40 seconds. Then, you rest, or drop to a low intensity for a similar interval before repeating.

The beauty of HIIT is being able to push yourself to your absolute limit, then recover just enough to go at 100% again – and again and again! It's those "just about get your breath back" rest intervals that allow you to recover, and then give it everything you've got once more.

Muscles are built while you sleep, not while you bench press, bicep curl or deadlift. By "nipping out" of your business on a regular basis, you'll return refreshed, re-energised and reinvigorated, full of ideas and inspiration, ready to give your business the very best of you.

After all, if your presence doesn't add value, your absence won't make a difference.

Sometimes (maybe even often), our businesses would be better off without us. Daniel Ek, founder of online music streaming pioneers Spotify, explains how he discovered this:

> *"After one of our product meetings, my Head of Product said to me: 'No one enjoys these meetings. You're not actually adding anything by being there'.*
>
> *My initial instinct was very defensive. But I decided to sleep on it. Eventually, I said, OK, let's see how well they do if I don't show up. And it turns out that they did incredibly well without me.*
>
> *I needed to figure out a way I could add value. Deciding if the button needed to be green or blue, or even if there needed to be a button at all – that's not where I added value.*
>
> *My value in that meeting was sharing context that they aren't aware of. Instead of pushing them towards a particular decision or sharing my preferences, it was about giving them context so that they can make better decisions as a team.*
>
> *That context could be insights I've gained from talking to other Silicon Valley CEOs who have found great ways to solve similar problems, or even why this is a worthwhile problem to solve in the first place."*

Just like Daniel, you'll give more value to your business by providing context and frameworks that enable your team to make better decisions, instead of making micro decisions for them.

Remember, with a False EXIT you'll remain as a shareholder and chief beneficiary of your business. Your name is at the very top of the new org chart. As shareholder, your duty is no longer to increase the profits of the business by carrying more buckets. Instead, it's to increase the value of the company by building a permanent, predictable pipeline that delivers sustainable, long-term profits.

It's important to understand the difference between a profit mindset and one focused on value. Patrick Bet-David, author of *Your Next Five Moves*, says: "Profit is about working in the business to make money. Value is working on the business to increase [shareholder] value. Profit is about instant gratification. Value is about delayed gratification. Profit is about sales mentality. Value is about CEO mentality."

I opened this chapter with a quote from Elon Musk, who testified in court that he didn't want to be the CEO of Tesla, Twitter, SpaceX, The Boring Company or indeed any of his business interests. One of the richest people on the planet, the vast majority of Musk's wealth comes from his shareholdings in those firms rather than any compensation he receives in salary or bonuses. Elon understands that the greatest value he can give to Tesla, for example, isn't to run the company well as CEO, but to invest his time (and unique way of thinking) into design and engineering.

Musk knows what he's good at and what he sucks at. He's aware of what he loves to do and what he hates. He leans in where he gives the greatest value and he lets go where he gives the least. This maximises the value long term for every shareholder – including Musk himself.

As a False EXIT-ed shareholder, my priority is to deliver shareholder value for the long term – ideally the rest of my life and beyond, as an asset my children and grandchildren could inherit. Having briefly tasted retirement aged 27, I'll likely never fully retire again. Why would I want to? As long as I can give value to the company and in return receive a sense of pride, purpose and fulfilment, this is a partnership that forms a virtuous circle – a perpetual flywheel to make Jim Collins proud.

Instead of retiring, I'll simply choose to "nip out" more frequently or for longer periods as I age. But as long as I can give value to the company, I've got a reason to get out of bed in the morning, as well as an excuse as to why my golf game isn't getting any better.

So how will you give the best value to your business? The answer may well be different for each and every reader. Like Daniel Ek, you need to discover what your greatest strength is – where you can add the greatest value to your company (without carrying buckets) that will increase shareholder value for you.

You may be an inspirational leader or a brilliant marketer. Perhaps you're a fantastic engineer, technician or manager. You could be the company's greatest strategist, able to create world class systems. Perhaps you're the face of the business, taking your brand to worldwide stages. A False EXIT encourages you to make your greatest strength your only role.

That could be the greatest gift you can give to your business.

9. I'M A BUSINESS OWNER, GET ME OUT OF HERE!

"Making a big life change is pretty scary. But you know what's even scarier? Regret,"

– Zig Ziglar

SCREW THIS, I'M OFF TO HAWAII

Henry Ford didn't build cars. He built factories.

Ray Kroc didn't sell burgers. He sold franchises.

From now on, you won't carry buckets. You'll build pipelines.

You'll be a business owner, not a business runner.

How many of us would be driving a Ford car today if Henry Ford insisted on personally hand-making each Model-T? And would we even have heard of McDonald's if Dick and Mac continued to run the business?

One of the first things Ray Kroc did to expand the McDonald's empire was to let those at the coal face make decisions. In his autobiography *Grinding It Out*, Kroc says: "I wanted the man closest to the stores to be able to make decisions without seeking directives from headquarters. I maintained that authority should go with a job. Some wrong decisions may be made as a result, but that's the only way you can encourage strong people to grow in an organisation."

Kroc understood the need to surrender control but only to the right people. He adds: "I once fired a member of our staff because he didn't wear the right kind of hat and didn't keep his shoes shined. I didn't like those things about the man, but those weren't the reasons I fired him. I just knew that he wasn't right for us. He was prone to making mistakes, and the hat and the shoes were merely symptoms of his sloppy way of thinking."

These high standards were a key foundation of the vision and values of McDonald's, with Kroc stressing the importance of "the fundamentals of Q, S, C and V" – quality, service, cleanliness and value – over and over again. He was similarly obsessed with simplifying each aspect of his highly systemised operation, making the decision-making framework for each employee far simpler. "Our stores were selling only nine items and they were buying only 35 or 40 items with which to make the nine."

This freed Kroc up to expand the McDonald's pipeline, smashing through his original target of opening a thousand restaurants, launching 7,500 by the time of his death in 1984, with Kroc's net worth estimated at $600million. Not bad for a milkshake salesman who never flipped a burger himself.

Growing a six-store enterprise into a huge multinational corporation is impressive. But what if your aspirations lie closer to home? What if building a personal fortune of several hundred million isn't your priority, but rather providing the best lifestyle possible for you and your family?

One Percenter Clarke Duncan founded affiliate marketing network Paid On Results in 2002. For a while, Clarke was very much the face of the business – attending every networking event, affiliate marketing conference and posting prolifically on industry message boards. Today though, Clarke isn't involved in the day-to-day operations. Instead, he set out his vision and values for the business, employed a small team of the right people, and equipped them with his decision-making framework, and robustly tested, highly optimised systems.

This enabled Clarke to emigrate to Spain with his family, where he launched a translation business – one that, again, didn't require Clarke for its day-to-day running. He then replicated the model, setting up a design agency and an outsourcing company in the Philippines for which he doesn't get dragged into any bucket-carrying duties, because he built the pipeline from day one.

Clarke recently returned to Scotland for family reasons. He can live anywhere in the world because he's not running the companies, carrying the buckets himself. Instead, he's improving the businesses, upgrading and refining their pipelines.

Clarke is a business owner in the true sense of the word. He's not a business runner. And neither am I.

I'm terrible at running businesses. I'm a weak leader and an irritating micro-manager. I have unrealistically high expectations of others and can't hide my displeasure when they fail to hit those expectations. I struggle to communicate things that come naturally to me and I'm more of a demotivator than a motivator.

Inspirational speeches? Getting the best out of my team? Being able to convince anybody to follow me into battle? Yeah, I'm nothing like that. I'm horrifyingly mediocre at running businesses.

It's a good job I own businesses, rather than run them then, isn't it? Remember my ideal job description?

> *"To do what I want...*
>
> *when I want...*

where I want…

how I want…

if I want!"

Well, I can't choose to only run my business when I want or if I feel like it!

If a customer calls and I don't answer the phone because I'm walking my dog in the countryside or stand-up paddleboarding along the coast, I won't be in business for long. But owning my business, putting the right people, frameworks, systems, and processes in place to run the business for me frees me up to truly do what I want, when I want, where I want, how I want – if I want!

A False EXIT gives you the ultimate freedom to enjoy owning (rather than running) your ambitious, lifestyle business. We all have those "I just can't do this anymore!" moments. Hopefully, it's just the odd bad day. But when those thoughts turn more prolonged, that's when you know you should have started planning your False EXIT a year earlier.

Derek Sivers, the founder of CD Baby – the online music publisher, distributor and retailer – used to hate going to the office. He found himself constantly bombarded with employees' questions. Unable to take any more, Derek seriously considered moving to Hawaii, changing his phone number, and not giving it to his staff. Instead, he built a team of the right people, who shared his vision and values. He invested a lot of time sharing his decision-making framework – explaining not just "What would Derek do?" but "Why would Derek do that?" – linking each decision back to his vision and values.

Derek created systems and processes, collated them all in a manual and found that he no longer hated going to the office. He was no longer distracted. His employees stopped asking questions. Because they had Derek's decision-making framework, they no longer needed the man himself. Derek could book a holiday to Hawaii any time he wanted, knowing his business was in safe hands. He could have taken a False EXIT. He actually ended up building a business that was insanely sellable (because he stopped running it and started owning it).

In 2008, Derek Sivers sold CD Baby for $22million. Not bad for a business that Derek would have fled to Hawaii to avoid running. (He then donated the lot to a charitable trust for music education – proving his vision and values were truly lived and breathed, and not just painted on the walls).

If the thought of changing your phone number, moving house, going away and not telling anyone where you've gone or when you'll be back (if ever) appeals to you, then it's definitely time to consider an exit plan. Remember, the exercise from the "How Will You Get Out?" section will show you what exit is best for you.

A GATEWAY DRUG FOR WORKAHOLICS

Here's a little exercise to see how ready you are to actually exit right now. For each statement below, rank your current situation on a scale of 1 to 5 (where 1 is weak and 5 is strong).

1. I have a clearly defined vision.
2. I have 3-5 clearly defined core values.
3. My core values are lived and breathed.
4. I have the right people on my bus.
5. I have ejected the wrong people from my bus.
6. I have the right people in the right seats.
7. I trust my people to make decisions (up to £______)
8. My people have access to (and use) my decision-making framework.
9. Everyone in the business knows our primary flywheel by heart.

10. The primary flywheel is turning efficiently.
11. The flywheel doesn't rely on me.
12. I have captured (and scored) my second-tier flywheels.
13. I have systems to ensure things run smoothly.
14. My systems are actually used.
15. I use red flag alerts to trust, yet verify.
16. I delegate, but don't abdicate.
17. I build pipelines, rather than carry buckets.
18. I know how to give the greatest value to my company.
19. I could take a 14-day holiday and leave my laptop/phone at home.
20. I don't run my business. I own my business.

Now add up your scores. Each 1 counts as 1 point, 2s give you 2 points, 3s are worth 3 points, and so on. There's a maximum score of 100, which gives you a percentage figure to indicate how ready you are to take a False EXIT.

Number of 1s	**Number of 2s**	**Number of 3s**	**Number of 4s**	**Number of 5s**
Multiply by 1	Multiply by 2	Multiply by 3	Multiply by 4	Multiply by 5

Now, the only place results come before work is in the dictionary, so don't be disheartened if you get a low score. This shows you where your pipeline needs work. Look back at any 1s and 2s you scored and think what needs to happen to turn them into 3s or 4s.

On the other hand, if you scored highly, why not consider taking a False EXIT for a test drive? You could start by simply working from home one day a week. You'll still be able to put out any fires that crop up, but you won't be in the office lighting them. If working from home goes well, why not take things a little further and plan a day off each week? Pick a day and tell everyone "I don't work Tuesdays", "I'm keeping Wednesdays client-free" or "Fridays are a family day from now on".

Then, if Won't Work Wednesday goes well, extend your test drive further. Take a week off. If you're feeling brave, try leaving the country (and your laptop/mobile phone at home). Once the thought of a week away from your business no longer brings you out in a cold sweat, try dialling it up to a fortnight, then a month and then a quarter.

A heads-up though: each time you extend the length of your exit, something will go wrong. Some fire prevention work will have been overlooked and cracks in the pipeline will make themselves known. It's similar to the "rule of three and ten" made famous by Hiroshi Mikitani, founder of Japan's largest e-commerce retailer, Rakuten. Mikitani found that everything breaks at predictable intervals when companies triple in size.

The systems you have as a solopreneur won't work with a team of three. The new three-person system works fine, until you reach ten employees, and then it's back to the drawing board for a new system. Same again when you reach 30 employees, 100, 300, etc. It's the same with the length of time you spend away from your business. Popping out for a day requires very little preparation, while taking a three day break does. That three-day prep won't be enough for a ten-day absence though and the ten-day system will break if you go swanning off for a month. The month-long setup won't work if you disappear on a three-month skive and even planning for a three-month absence won't show up the cracks and problems that a year-long sabbatical would.

Mere paragraphs ago, I was twisting your arm to consider working from home one day a week and now I'm suggesting you could take a year off. Well, time away from your business can be a gateway drug in itself. Many former workaholics discover a newfound lust for life outside of work when they step off the hamster wheel and consciously plan what they want out of life. Their time in work suddenly becomes more fulfilling, with less draining day-to-day drudgery. And their time out of work becomes invigorating, with the freedom to truly live their best life.

So what will you do with this new-found free time? Will you finally make your health a priority? Will Tuesday afternoons be "date night" for you and your partner, with the cinema to yourselves (and the two-for-one lunch deal at your favourite restaurant)? Why not take your kids to the park? Or spend some time with your parents? Learn that new skill. Take up that hobby you've always fancied. Start a new business or write that book that's been inside you all these years. You might even improve your golf handicap!

Consider me the mischievous kid, making faces at the classroom window, encouraging you to skive off and have some fun, instead of updating your privacy policy, reconciling your bank statements or whatever mundane task you had planned.

As Ferriss Bueller, the king of knocking off early, says: "The question isn't 'What are we going to do?'. The question is 'What *aren't* we going to do?'."

10. CONCLUSION

> *"Have your cake and eat it... there's no other reason to have a cake,"*
>
> *– Derren Brown*

Will you still be running your business when you're 96?

Elizabeth did.

It wasn't because she needed the money (she was one of the wealthiest people in the country).

It wasn't because there was no one else to delegate to. She had children and grandchildren who could have taken over the firm decades earlier.

She wasn't even in the best of health. She suffered from severely restricted mobility and had recently been widowed. But Elizabeth was determined to continue running her organisation well into her mid-90s simply because she made a promise to do so when she was 25.

This was a promise Elizabeth (or Her Majesty Queen Elizabeth II, to use her better-known title) kept, fulfilling her duties until the day she died, on September 8th, 2022.

Elizabeth was head of the British Royal Family for more than seven decades, becoming the longest reigning monarch in history. As the figurehead of her organisation, she remained in the top position until her death, aged 96.

I just asked if you would still be running your business aged 96. Perhaps a better question is how could you still "run" your business aged 96? By now, I'd hope you know the answer – to be a business owner, not a business runner. The transition from running a business to owning a business is one that can happen gradually, over time.

When I was a kid, the Queen used to be incredibly active. She would spend long days touring the country, meeting her subjects (customers), opening hospitals, and traipsing around factories, smelling fresh paint everywhere she went, being presented with yet another posy of flowers, and asking, "And what do you do?" hundreds of times a day.

Slowly but steadily though, Elizabeth started to remove herself from the day-to-day operations – delegating duties such as the FA Cup presentation or the opening of less prestigious public buildings to others. Gradually, she began to carry fewer buckets herself, increasingly delegating responsibilities to more junior members of the family. Years before King Charles III ascended to the throne, the then-Prince of Wales grew accustomed to knighting the great and the good of British society, as well as rolling out the red carpet for visiting dignitaries, presidents, and overseas royalty. He even read the Queen's speech at the State Opening of Parliament, accompanied by the Imperial State Crown.

However, Elizabeth remained the figurehead – it was her face on the stamps and coins. Nine million people watched her final Christmas Day speech in 2021. She remained the focal point of ceremonial events such as the State Opening of Parliament, Trooping the Colour, and the Royal Maundy Service. These were duties that Her Majesty fulfilled, until poor health prevented her from doing so.

By September 6th, 2022, Elizabeth was becoming more and more frail. Public appearances had become a thing of the past. Never one to neglect her duties, however, Elizabeth rose from her sick bed at Balmoral, welcoming incoming Prime Minister Liz Truss, asking her to form a government on her behalf. Just 48 hours later, the new PM stood on the steps of Downing Street to announce the passing of Her Majesty Queen Elizabeth II.

Elizabeth found a way to continue running her organisation right up until her death. She had very clearly demonstrated core values – those of service, dedication, and dignity – which, of course, were lived and breathed, not just painted on the walls. Over 70 years, she never once wavered from her values as a person, nor her vision for her country.

You can't choose your family of course, but Elizabeth still surrounded herself with the right people – trusted advisors and loyal household staff. At her state funeral, Paul Whybrew, one of the Queen's most trusted staff members, walked ahead of Her Majesty's hearse. Elizabeth valued her relationship with him highly. They would spend hours watching sport together at Balmoral, and Elizabeth personally paid for Paul's Windsor flat to be renovated so he could move to be closer to her.

Alongside Whybrew was Matthew Magee – the Queen's private secretary. Having Whybrew and Magee accompany her coffin (as her husband Prince Phillip requested senior household staff do at his funeral), Elizabeth once again demonstrated the importance of surrounding yourself with the right people.

Of course, Her Majesty also brought inspirational leadership to the organisation, together with a very clear decision-making framework (handed down from generation to generation). Anyone watching the Queen's funeral (it's claimed more than five billion people worldwide did just that on television) will have witnessed the many systems at work within the Royal Family – the tradition, the pomp, the ceremony. Everything executed with military precision.

More than anything though, Elizabeth knew how she could give the greatest value to her organisation. She understood the need for her role to evolve over seven decades, from extremely active working royal to symbolic figurehead, via ever increasing delegation but never abdication.

So, how could you still run your business aged 96?

By delegating, not abdicating.

By having clearly defined vision and values, which are lived and breathed by the right people, armed with your decision-making framework and systems to trust yet verify.

By building pipelines rather than carrying buckets.

By taking a False EXIT.

You've read the book. Now it's time to follow the instructions. Information on its own is worthless. Combined with implementation, it is priceless.

It's time to put down those buckets and start building your pipeline. Ready?

Go.

RESOURCES

You can access all of the resources mentioned in this book at www.bigidea.co.uk/falseexit, including:

- A blank "Which EXIT should I take?" weighted pros/cons template.
- A 54-minute False EXIT Masterclass.
- An interview with Exeter Chiefs' Rob Baxter, describing the ACE framework.
- Guy Singh-Watson's full Founder's Wishes document.
- Warren Buffett's "Berkshire – Past, Present and Future" letter to shareholders.
- How Barack Obama approached POTUS-level decisions.
- An interview with Neville Wright on his £70million exit.
- A create-your-own Flywheel template.
- My Actual Hourly Rate calculator
- An interview with me – John Lamerton – describing my many failed attempts to exit my business, before discovering the False EXIT.

And if you have any further questions or would like a pointer on the topics covered in this book, please email john@bigidea.co.uk.

ABOUT THE AUTHOR

John Lamerton is a serial entrepreneur and investor, a former civil servant who started a dotcom company in 2000, despite having no skills, knowledge or experience – "but then neither did most of the other dotcom businesses at that time, so I was in good company!"

He's owned a website that told students where to get free sachets of shampoo, one that told people they'd been caught speeding (when they hadn't), and one that told football fans where to get the best pies.

Before he knew it, he was running a dating website, selling office space, working with florists to sell online, and selling package holidays to the Algarve. He's also owned a bingo website, a finance blog, sold mobile phone insurance, and streamed live sports events. Trust me, that's the short version too – John's owned or operated more than 100 businesses in a wide variety of sectors.

Since exiting the day-to-day running of his businesses in 2016, John spends his days coaching ambitious, lifestyle business owners. Together with Jason Brockman, his business partner of more than two decades, John runs a paid group-coaching programme (The One Percent Club), and hosts a free podcast. You can find details of both at www.bigidea.co.uk.

A perennial optimist, John firmly believes that the "mighty" Plymouth Argyle will one day play in the top-tier of English football. He lives in Devon with his wife Sarah and two children, Jack and Harrie.

He's a bit of a fanboy of Warren Buffett.

And he can always, *always* be bribed with cake. Or a cream tea. Just remember he's from Devon, so it's cream first!

ALSO BY JOHN LAMERTON

Big Ideas... for Small Businesses

The blueprint for running a successful, ambitious, lifestyle business. Centred around John's ideal job description: "To do *what* I want, *when* I want, *how* I want, *where* I want... *if* I want", *Big Ideas...* is full of simple, practical tools and tactics to help your small business grow.

Available in Paperback, Kindle and Audiobook (narrated by John).

Routine Machine

Consistency is a superpower. In *Routine Machine*, John explains how a "normal bloke from Plymouth" achieved more success than he ever dreamed (or deserved) by following a simple, everyday plan to achieve his goals that required neither superhuman effort nor natural-born talent (which is just as well).

Available in Paperback, Kindle and Audiobook (narrated by John).

Evergreen Assets

The "do the work once, reap the rewards again and again (and again!)" content marketing ecosystem. Evergreen Assets is a complete "swipe and deploy" ecosystem for running almost any business – centred on permanent "evergreen" marketing assets that enable you to work less and earn more.

Available in Paperback, Kindle and Audiobook (narrated by John).

BIBLIOGRAPHY

Abrashoff, C. D. (2002). *It's Your Ship: Management Techniques from the Best Damn Ship in the Navy.* New York: Grand Central Publishing.

Beaman, A., Klentz, B., Diener, E., & Svanum, S. (1979). Self-awareness and transgression in children: Two field studies. *Journal of Personality and Social Psychology.*

Bet-David, P. (2020). *Your Next Five Moves: Master the Art of Business Strategy.* New York: Gallery Books.

Catalano, F., & Smith, B. E. (2000). *Internet Marketing for Dummies.* New York: John Wiley & Sons.

Clear, J. (2018). *Atomic Habits: An Easy & Proven Way to Build Good Habits & Break Bad Ones.* New York: Random House Business.

Collins, J. (2001). *Good To Great: Why Some Companies Make the Leap... and Others Don't.* New York: Random House Business.

Collins, J. (2019). *Turning the Flywheel: A Monograph to Accompany Good to Great.* New York: Harper Business.

Gerber, M. (1986). *The E-Myth : Why Most Small Businesses Don't Work and What to Do About It.* Harper.

Hsieh, T. (2010). *Delivering Happiness: A Path to Profits, Passion and Purpose.* New York: Grand Central Publishing.

Isaacson, W. (2011). *Steve Jobs: The Exclusive Biography.* New York: Simon & Schuster.

Kroc, R. (1977). *Grinding It Out: The Making Of McDonald's.* New York: St. Martin's Press.

Lamerton, J. (2017). *Big Ideas... For Small Businesses: Simple, Practical Tools and Tactics to Help Your Small Business.* Let's Tell Your Story Publishing.

Lamerton, J. (2019). *Routine Machine: How successful people improve their morning routine, daily habits and guarantee themselves results.* Let's Tell Your Story Publishing.

Sinek, S. (2011). *Start With Why: How Great Leaders Inspire Everyone To Take Action.* London: Penguin.

Singh-Watson, G. (2018). *Vegetables, Soil & Hope: Ruminations of a life long veg nerd.* Riverford Organic Farms.

Stone, B. (2013). *The Everything Store: Jeff Bezos and the Age of Amazon.* Boston, MA: Little, Brown.

Printed in Great Britain
by Amazon

25386771R00119